BEST OF
STEAK

GARDEN *of* **GRAPES.**

Introduction

Ladies and gentlemen, fellow connoisseurs of carnivorous delight, and all you hungry souls yearning for that perfect sear – welcome. Here we stand at the threshold of a gastronomic globe-trot, a voyage that promises to take your taste buds on a journey through the sizzling symphonies of steak, the culinary cornerstone that unites tables across continents.

Consider this not just a cookbook, but your passport to a world of succulent exploration. In "Best of Steak: Around the World in 120 Steaks," we've embarked on a mission to bring the planet's finest cuts, flavors, and techniques right to your kitchen. Buckle up, my friends, because we're about to traverse the continents, savoring every bite and learning from every sizzle.

With the flicker of flames and the seductive scent of searing meat as our backdrop, let's dive into the heart of this carnivore's dream. But first, allow me to share what fueled my desire to create this culinary compendium.

The inspiration? It's a tale woven from the threads of exploration, curiosity, and the shared joy of breaking bread – or should I say, cutting steak? Through bustling Argentine parrillas, bustling Tokyo yakitori stalls, and bustling American backyard barbecues, I've tasted the camaraderie that accompanies every perfectly grilled piece of meat. It's the art of bringing people together, transcending language barriers with the universal language of deliciousness.

So, what can you expect from this journey? Imagine flipping through pages that span continents, each recipe unveiling a new facet of steak's enchanting versatility. From the robust simplicity of a Texan ribeye to the delicate refinement of a Japanese Wagyu, we're celebrating the diversity that lies within the realm of beef. But it's not just about cuts; it's about cultures, traditions, and the artistry of flavors that evolve as we cross borders.

As you embark on this culinary odyssey, rest assured that you're not alone. With detailed step-by-step instructions, vibrant photographs that'll practically make you taste the steak through the page, and anecdotes that let you peek into the kitchens of the world, we're your co-pilots on this adventure.

So, sharpen those knives, stoke those fires, and prepare your palate for a journey that promises to be as rich and nuanced as the flavors that grace your plate. Let's go beyond the well-done and rare, and discover the steak stories that feed the soul. Welcome to "Best of Steak." It's time to fire up the grill and ignite your appetite for the world's favorite fare.

Cooking Philosophy or Approach

Now, before we set out on this carnivorous escapade, let's talk about the heart and soul that infuse these recipes. My approach to cooking and food is a blend of reverence and rebellion, a celebration of tradition and a dance with innovation.

For me, cooking is more than a transaction of sustenance; it's an intimate conversation with ingredients. Each cut of meat tells a story, and every technique is a dialogue between cook and kitchen. From the primal thrill of a perfectly seasoned rub to the intricacies of mastering the flame's embrace, I see cooking as an art form that paints the palate with every brushstroke.

In these recipes, you won't find rigid rules, but rather a roadmap for exploration. Yes, a steak can stand alone, its natural flavors singing in unison, but it's also a canvas for global influence. Expect the bold, smoky strokes of a Texan dry rub, the elegant subtlety of a French bordelaise, and the captivating complexity of Asian marinades. These techniques are our passport to the steak symphonies that echo worldwide.

But let's talk about the star of our show – the beef itself. It's more than a protein; it's an embodiment of terroir, a reflection of the land it grazed upon. Whether you're grilling, searing, or slow-cooking, it's essential to respect the meat's journey from pasture to plate. It's the reason behind my insistence on quality cuts, the reverence for the marbling that promises an unforgettably tender experience.

Now, when it comes to ingredients, think of this cookbook as a market where cultures collide. We'll dance with spices that span continents, herbs that whisper secrets, and sauces that sing stories. And as we infuse these recipes with global flavors, remember – my recipes are a guide, not a commandment. Don't hesitate to deviate, to add your own twist. Cooking is, after all, an intimate affair, and your taste buds are the ultimate judges.

So, my fellow steak enthusiasts, grab your aprons, wield your tongs, and let's set the grill ablaze with flavor. In these pages, we're not just cooking steak; we're capturing memories, celebrating traditions, and forging new culinary narratives. Get ready to travel through time zones and taste profiles, because with "Best of Steak," every meal is a ticket to the world's most mouthwatering destinations.

Italian Truffle-Infused Ribeye
See Page, 73

General Cooking Tips and Techniques

Ah, my fellow grill masters and steak aficionados, before you embark on this carnivorous journey, let's lay down some cooking wisdom that'll make your culinary creations sing like a sizzling serenade.

1. Temperature Tango: When it comes to grilling, searing, or roasting, temperature is your guiding star. A trusty meat thermometer is your sidekick, ensuring you hit that perfect point of juicy tenderness.

2. Rest and Relaxation: Patience, my friends, is a virtue when it comes to steak. After cooking, let your meat rest. It's like a post-travel siesta for your cut, allowing the juices to redistribute for maximum flavor.

3. Seasoning Sutra: Never underestimate the power of seasoning. A well-balanced rub or marinade can elevate your steak from good to glorious. Salt isn't just a seasoning; it's a seasoning ritual. Sprinkle with purpose and watch the magic unfold.

4. The Heat Dance: Whether you're searing on high heat or slow-roasting, remember the heat dance. Sear to lock in flavors, then lower the heat for a leisurely cooking journey. Think of it as a steak tango – a fiery embrace followed by a gentle sway.

5. Oil and the Art of Basting: Basting isn't just for the pros. Regular basting with a mix of oil, butter, and aromatics is like giving your steak a spa treatment, ensuring it stays moist and infused with flavor.

6. Precision Prep: Prep like a pro – take the time to bring your steak to room temperature before cooking. It's like giving it a warm hug before it hits the heat.

7. Keep it Clean: A clean grill is a happy grill. Scrub those grates, brush them with oil, and let your steak meet the grill with a non-stick embrace.

8. The Flip Game: One flip, two flip, three flip, done! Don't get too flip-happy with your steak. Allow it to sear on each side, building up those glorious grill marks and a caramelized crust.

Advice on Ingredient Selection, Preparation, and Cooking Methods:

Cuts of Glory: Choose your cut wisely. Different cuts offer different flavors and textures. Go for ribeyes if you crave marbling, or opt for tenderloins for a lean, melt-in-your-mouth experience.

Quality Matters: Quality trumps all. Invest in well-sourced, properly aged beef. The difference in taste is like comparing a harmonious symphony to a discordant note.

Prep School: Before grilling, pat your steak dry. Moisture on the surface can hinder that perfect sear you're aiming for.

Marination Magic: Marinades aren't just flavor; they're tenderizers. The acids in marinades can work wonders on tougher cuts, ensuring a juicy end result.

Restful Bliss: After cooking, allow your steak to rest. This lets the juices redistribute, resulting in a more succulent bite.

Slice with Precision: When you're ready to slice, do it with purpose. Go against the grain for tender cuts, and let those knife skills shine.

Spice Spectrum: Experiment with spices from different corners of the world. Embrace the smoky, the spicy, the sweet – let your taste buds explore.

Slow and Steady: Don't rush the process. Slow-cooked steaks can unlock layers of flavor, showcasing the steak's potential in a whole new light.

Remember, my meat-loving comrades, you hold the reins to your steak destiny. With a little technique, a dash of creativity, and a whole lot of sizzle, you're ready to embark on a culinary voyage that promises to leave your taste buds longing for more. So, sharpen those knives, dust off that apron, and let's get cooking – the world's finest steaks await your culinary prowess.

Brazilian Bacon-Wrapped Ribeye
See Page, 55

Kitchen Essentials

Ahoy, culinary adventurers! Before you dive into the world of steaks, let's make sure you're armed with the right tools – your trusty companions as you embark on this meaty escapade.

1. Grill Pan: Your trusty ally for achieving those iconic grill marks without the need for an actual grill. Preheat it well, oil those ridges, and let the sizzling spectacle begin.

2. Cast Iron Skillet: The workhorse of your kitchen. A well-seasoned cast iron skillet is your go-to for searing, browning, and imparting that mouthwatering crust.

3. Meat Thermometer: This is your steak's guardian angel. Whether you're aiming for rare, medium, or well-done, a meat thermometer ensures you hit the bullseye every time.

4. Tongs: A sturdy pair of tongs is your extension of hands. They help you flip, turn, and maneuver steaks on the grill or in the pan.

5. Chef's Knife: Precision is key, and a sharp chef's knife is your best tool for slicing, dicing, and trimming your cuts to perfection.

6. Cutting Board: Give your steaks a stage to shine on – a spacious cutting board that can handle the juices and the slicing action.

7. Meat Pounder: When you need to tenderize or even out the thickness of your steaks, a meat pounder is your secret weapon.

8. Basting Brush: Anointed with marinades and bastes, the basting brush ensures your steaks get an extra layer of flavor love.

9. Ovenproof Pan: For those times when you need to finish off your steak in the oven, an ovenproof pan is your trusty partner.

10. Timer: Don't rely on memory when perfection is at stake. A timer keeps you on point, ensuring your steaks are cooked to your preferred level.

11. Oil Brush: A silicone oil brush is your paintbrush for grilling. It lets you coat your steaks evenly with oil for that golden sear.

Tips on How to Use These Tools Effectively:

Preheat Like a Pro: Whether it's your grill pan or cast iron skillet, preheating is crucial. It ensures that sizzle when your steak hits the surface.

Get a Handle on Tongs: Use tongs instead of a fork to flip your steaks. Piercing the meat with a fork lets those precious juices escape.

Mind the Meat Thermometer: Insert the meat thermometer into the thickest part of the steak, away from bone or fat. And make sure not to touch the pan or grill grates – you're measuring the meat, not the surface.

Cast Iron Love: Season your cast iron skillet well and maintain that seasoning for the ultimate non-stick surface.

Rest for Success: After cooking, let your steaks rest. A few minutes can make all the difference, resulting in a more flavorful and tender bite.

Watch the Clock: Timing is your ally. Different thicknesses and cooking methods require different cooking times. Use your timer to keep track.

Basting Brilliance: When basting, use your brush to apply the marinade or oil evenly. It's like giving your steak a flavor hug.

Clean Up with Care: Cast iron needs a little TLC. After use, wipe it down with a cloth and avoid soap – a rinse and a gentle scrub will do the trick.

With these kitchen essentials by your side and the knowledge to wield them effectively, you're all set to conquer the steak domain like a true culinary maestro. So, fire up that grill pan, embrace the sizzle, and let the aromas of perfectly cooked steaks waft through your kitchen – you've got this!

Turkish Yogurt-Marinated Sirloin
See Page, 13

Flavor Pairing Suggestions

Ahoy, flavor voyagers! As we sail through the sea of steaks, it's time to sprinkle a little creativity onto your culinary canvas. Here are some flavor pairing inspirations that'll awaken the artist within you, urging you to create your steak masterpieces.

1. Herbaceous Elegance: Elevate your steak with the fragrant embrace of fresh herbs. Thyme and rosemary lend a rustic charm, while cilantro and mint bring a burst of vibrancy. Create your own herb-infused rubs or finish your steak with a sprinkle of finely chopped greens.

2. Fruity Fusion: A splash of fruity goodness can work wonders. Pair juicy peaches with grilled steak for a sweet-savory dance, or experiment with a drizzle of pomegranate molasses to awaken your taste buds.

3. Umami Unveiled: Unleash the umami magic with ingredients like mushrooms, soy sauce, and miso. These savory powerhouses can take your steak from delicious to unforgettable.

4. Tangy Temptations: A tangy twist can cut through the richness of steak. Think pickled red onions or a squeeze of lemon to balance the flavors and add a zesty kick.

5. Spices of the World: Embark on a global spice journey. Dive into the smoky allure of paprika, explore the warm depths of cumin, or let a touch of curry powder transport you to distant lands.

6. Creamy Indulgences: Indulge in the velvety embrace of sauces. A dollop of blue cheese or a drizzle of garlic aioli can add a luscious layer to your steak experience.

7. Nutty Nuances: Nuts bring a satisfying crunch and nutty undertone. Try crushed pistachios for a textural contrast or sprinkle toasted almonds for a hint of earthy flavor.

8. Wine and Dine: A wine reduction can elevate your steak to elegance. Red wine pairs beautifully with hearty cuts, while white wine sauces add a touch of refinement to lighter options.

9. A Touch of Heat: For those who crave the fiery embrace, introduce chili flakes or hot sauce. A kick of heat can awaken dormant flavors and send your taste buds on a spicy adventure.

10. Earthy Richness: Delve into the earthy wonders of roasted garlic or caramelized onions. These elements can bring a depth of flavor that complements the steak's robust profile.

Remember, my fellow culinary explorers, these pairings are merely guiding stars. Feel free to mix and match, experiment, and craft your own symphonies of flavor. The kitchen is your playground, and your taste buds are the ultimate judges. So, embrace your inner flavor artist, let your imagination run wild, and let each bite of steak tell a story as unique as your palate. Bon appétit, and may your flavor adventures be as bold as your appetite!

INDEX

Chapter 1:
Ribeye Delights

1
person

600
calories

15
minutes

American BBQ Ribeye Steak

Ingredients:

- 1 Ribeye steak (1 inch thick)
- Salt and pepper to taste
- 1 tsp paprika
- Tangy BBQ sauce for serving

Ah, the iconic taste of freedom – the American BBQ Ribeye Steak. Born beneath open skies and nurtured by fiery grills, this dish boasts bold flavors that stand as a testament to the land of the brave.
Fire up the grill, season the meat with salt, pepper, and a hint of paprika. Grill each side for about 4-5 minutes for a medium-rare masterpiece. Let it rest, then slice and serve with a side of tangy BBQ sauce.
Let the stars and stripes guide your taste buds!

Directions

1. Fire up the grill to medium-high heat.
2. Season the ribeye with salt, pepper, and paprika on both sides.
3. Grill the steak for 4-5 minutes on each side for medium-rare.
4. Remove from the grill and let it rest for a few minutes.
5. Slice against the grain and serve with BBQ sauce.

1
person

550
calories

20
minutes

French Peppercorn-Crusted Filet Mignon

Ingredients:

- 1 Filet Mignon steak
- Salt to taste
- 2 tbsp black peppercorns, crushed
- 1 tbsp olive oil
- 1/2 cup red wine
- 1/4 cup beef broth
- 1 shallot, minced

In the heart of Parisian romance, this Peppercorn-Crusted Filet Mignon was conceived. The elegant dance of tender meat and fiery peppercorns creates a symphony of flavors that charms even the most discerning palates.
Crush black peppercorns and press onto the filet. Sear each side in a hot pan, then finish in the oven. Serve with a luscious red wine reduction. For love and cuisine, the French know the way.

Directions

1. Preheat the oven to 400°F (200°C).
2. Season the filet with salt and press the crushed peppercorns onto both sides.
3. Heat oil in an oven-safe pan and sear the steak for 2-3 minutes per side.
4. Transfer to the oven and roast for 5-7 minutes for medium-rare.
5. In the same pan, sauté shallots. Pour in wine and broth, simmer.
6. Serve the filet with the wine reduction.

2 tacos

450
calories

25
minutes

Mexican Ribeye Tacos with Salsa Verde

Ingredients:

- 1 Ribeye steak, sliced
- Juice of 2 limes
- 1 tsp ground cumin
- 2 cloves garlic, minced
- Salt and pepper to taste
- 4 small flour tortillas
- Salsa verde
- Chopped onions and cilantro for topping

A fiesta of flavors awaits with these Mexican Ribeye Tacos. Born on the streets of Mexico, these tender ribeye strips are nestled in warm tortillas, adorned with vibrant salsa verde.
Marinate ribeye in lime juice, cumin, and garlic. Sear until juicy and slice. Serve in tortillas with salsa verde, onions, and cilantro.
Spice up your life with each bite!

Directions

1. In a bowl, combine lime juice, cumin, garlic, salt, and pepper.
2. Marinate the sliced ribeye in this mixture for 15 minutes.
3. Heat a pan and cook the ribeye until browned and juicy.
4. Warm the tortillas and fill with the ribeye.
5. Top with salsa verde, onions, and cilantro.

 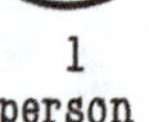  

1
person

620
calories

30
minutes

Brazilian Chimichurri-Marinated Ribeye

Ingredients:

- 1 Ribeye steak
- Salt and pepper to taste
- 1 cup fresh parsley
- 4 cloves garlic
- 1 tsp dried oregano
- 1/2 cup red wine vinegar
- 1/4 cup olive oil

From the lush lands of Brazil comes the Chimichurri-Marinated Ribeye. Bathed in a zesty herb sauce, this ribeye sings with flavors of garlic, parsley, and tangy vinegar.
Blend parsley, garlic, oregano, and vinegar for the marinade. Grill the ribeye to perfection and serve with an extra drizzle of chimichurri.
Taste the Amazon rainforest on a plate!

Directions

1. In a blender, combine parsley, garlic, oregano, vinegar, salt, and pepper.
2. Blend while drizzling in olive oil.
3. Season the ribeye with salt and grill to your preference.
4. Drizzle chimichurri over the grilled steak.

1
person

580
calories

45
minutes

Greek Grilled Beef Moussaka

Ingredients:

- 1/2 lb ground beef
- 1 onion, chopped
- 2 cloves garlic, minced
- 1 tsp ground cinnamon
- 1/2 tsp ground allspice
- 1 can crushed tomatoes
- 1 large eggplant, sliced
- 1/4 cup butter
- 1/4 cup all-purpose flour
- 2 cups milk
- 1/4 cup grated Parmesan cheese

From the sun-kissed shores of Greece emerges the Grilled Beef Moussaka. Layered with history and flavor, this dish melds rich ground beef with creamy béchamel and earthy eggplant.
Brown beef with onions, add spices, tomatoes. Layer beef, eggplant, and béchamel. Bake to perfection.
Savor the Mediterranean breeze on your plate!

Directions

1. In a pan, brown beef with onions and garlic.
2. Add cinnamon, allspice, salt, and pepper. Stir in tomatoes, simmer.
3. In a separate pan, melt butter, stir in flour. Gradually whisk in milk.
4. Layer eggplant, beef mixture, and béchamel in a baking dish.
5. Top with Parmesan and bake at 350°F (175°C) until golden.

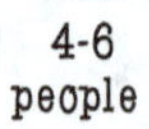

4-6
people

500
calories

10
minutes

Italian Rosemary
Ribeye Roast

Ingredients:

- 1 Ribeye roast (3-4 lbs)
- Salt and pepper to taste
- 4 cloves garlic, minced
- 3 tbsp fresh rosemary, chopped
- 2 tbsp olive oil
- 4 large potatoes, peeled and quartered

In the heart of Italy, the Rosemary Ribeye Roast was born. This aromatic masterpiece brings together succulent ribeye and fragrant rosemary, creating an unforgettable symphony of taste. Rub ribeye with rosemary, garlic, olive oil. Roast to perfection. Slice and serve with roasted potatoes.
Let the Italian hills come alive on your palate!

Directions

1. Preheat oven to 450°F (230°C).
2. Mix garlic, rosemary, olive oil, salt, and pepper.
3. Rub the mixture over the ribeye.
4. Place the roast on a rack in a roasting pan, surrounded by potatoes.
5. Roast for 20 minutes, then reduce the temperature to 350°F (175°C).
6. Roast until desired doneness, let it rest before slicing.

1
person

600
calories

35
minutes

Moroccan Ras El Hanout Ribeye

Ingredients:

- 1 Ribeye steak
- Salt and pepper to taste
- 2 tbsp ras el hanout spice blend
- 1 cup couscous
- Fresh mint leaves for garnish
- Greek yogurt mixed with chopped mint

From the spice-scented bazaars of Morocco comes the Ras El Hanout Ribeye. This dish captures the essence of North Africa, blending the aromatic charm of ras el hanout with the succulence of ribeye.
Coat ribeye with ras el hanout. Sear, then roast. Serve with couscous and mint yogurt.
Embark on a flavorful journey across the desert dunes!

Directions

1. Rub the ribeye with salt, pepper, and ras el hanout.
2. Sear the steak in a hot pan.
3. Roast in the oven until desired doneness.
4. Prepare the couscous according to package instructions.
5. Serve the ribeye slices with couscous, mint yogurt, and fresh mint.

 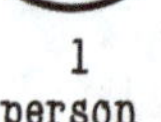  

1
person

530
calories

40
minutes

Japanese Miso-Marinated Ribeye

Ingredients:

- 1 Ribeye steak
- Salt and pepper to taste
- 1/4 cup white miso paste
- 1/4 cup sake
- 2 tbsp mirin
- 1 tbsp sugar
- Steamed rice and pickled vegetables for serving

Inspired by the Land of the Rising Sun, the Miso-Marinated Ribeye offers a harmonious blend of umami and tenderness. With a miso-infused marinade, this dish pays homage to Japanese culinary finesse.
Mix miso, sake, mirin, sugar. Marinate ribeye. Grill to perfection. Serve with steamed rice and pickled vegetables.
Let your taste buds journey to Japan!

Directions

1. In a bowl, whisk miso, sake, mirin, and sugar.
2. Marinate the ribeye for 30 minutes.
3. Grill the steak to your liking.
4. Serve with steamed rice and pickled vegetables.

1
person

570
calories

50
minutes

Korean Soy-Ginger Glazed Ribeye

Ingredients:

- 1 Ribeye steak
- Salt and pepper to taste
- 1/4 cup soy sauce
- 2 tbsp brown sugar
- 2 cloves garlic, minced
- 1 tbsp grated ginger
- Steamed bok choy and kimchi for serving

From the vibrant streets of Seoul comes the Soy-Ginger Glazed Ribeye. This dish marries the boldness of Korean flavors with the elegance of ribeye.
Marinate ribeye in soy, ginger, and garlic. Grill to perfection. Serve with steamed bok choy and kimchi.
Let the K-pop of flavors explode in your mouth!

Directions

1. In a bowl, mix soy sauce, brown sugar, garlic, and ginger.
2. Marinate the ribeye for 40 minutes.
3. Grill the steak until caramelized.
4. Serve with steamed bok choy and kimchi.

1
person

490
calories

20
minutes

Argentinean Chimichurri Flat Iron

Ingredients:

- 1 Flat Iron steak
- Salt and pepper to taste
- 1 cup fresh parsley
- 4 cloves garlic
- 1/4 cup red wine vinegar
- 1/2 cup olive oil

Straight from the pampas of Argentina, the Chimichurri Flat Iron delights with a burst of tangy and herby goodness. A match made in gaucho heaven – flat iron steak and chimichurri sauce.
Blend parsley, garlic, vinegar. Grill flat iron and serve with chimichurri.
Let the spirit of the Argentinean countryside fill your plate!

Directions

1. In a blender, combine parsley, garlic, vinegar, salt, and pepper.
2. Blend while drizzling in olive oil.
3. Season the flat iron steak with salt and pepper.
4. Grill until medium-rare.
5. Serve the steak with a generous drizzle of chimichurri sauce.

Chapter 2:
Sirloin Sensations

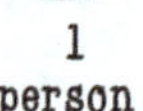

1
person

540
calories

35
minutes

Turkish Yogurt-Marinated Sirloin

Ingredients:

- 1 Sirloin steak
- Salt and pepper to taste
- 1 cup Greek yogurt
- 3 cloves garlic, minced
- 1 tsp paprika
- 1 tsp cumin
- Flatbread and tzatziki for serving

From the bustling markets of Istanbul emerges the Yogurt-Marinated Sirloin. This Turkish delight combines the tang of yogurt and the richness of sirloin.

Marinate sirloin in yogurt, garlic, spices. Grill to perfection. Serve with flatbread and a dollop of tzatziki.

Let the mystique of the Bosphorus infuse your palate!

Directions

1. In a bowl, mix yogurt, garlic, paprika, cumin, salt, and pepper.
2. Marinate the sirloin in this mixture for 30 minutes.
3. Grill the steak until nicely charred and cooked.
4. Slice and serve with warm flatbread and a dollop of tzatziki.

1
person

620
calories

40
minutes

Spanish Galician T-Bone

Ingredients:

- 1 T-Bone steak
- Salt to taste
- Olive oil for rubbing
- Patatas bravas for serving

Straight from the heart of Spain, the Galician T-Bone is a testament to the rustic charm of Spanish cuisine. This dish showcases the flavors of premium T-bone steak with a simple rub of olive oil and sea salt.
Rub T-bone with olive oil, sea salt. Grill to perfection. Serve with patatas bravas.
Let the spirit of Spain dance on your taste buds!

Directions

1. Preheat the grill to high heat.
2. Rub the T-bone steak with olive oil and generously season with salt.
3. Grill the steak to your preferred doneness.
4. Let it rest before slicing.
5. Serve with crispy patatas bravas for an authentic Spanish experience.

2
fajitas

460
calories

30
minutes

Mexican Carne Asada Fajitas

Ingredients:

- 1 Sirloin steak, sliced
- Juice of 2 limes
- 3 cloves garlic, minced
- 1 tsp chili powder
- 1 tsp cumin
- Salt and pepper to taste
- 1 red bell pepper, sliced
- 1 green bell pepper, sliced
- 1 onion, sliced
- Flour tortillas for serving

Inspired by the streets of Mexico, Carne Asada Fajitas are a burst of colors and flavors. This dish fuses marinated sirloin with vibrant peppers and onions, offering a fiesta on a plate.
Marinate sirloin in lime juice, garlic, spices. Sear with peppers and onions. Serve with warm tortillas.
Let the Mariachi tunes accompany your feast!

Directions

1. In a bowl, mix lime juice, garlic, chili powder, cumin, salt, and pepper.
2. Marinate the sliced sirloin for 20 minutes.
3. Sear the marinated sirloin in a hot pan.
4. Add sliced peppers and onions, sauté until tender.
5. Serve the mixture in warm flour tortillas.

1
person

490
calories

25
minutes

Italian Balsamic Glazed Sirloin

Ingredients:

- 1 Sirloin steak
- Salt and pepper to taste
- 1/4 cup balsamic vinegar
- 2 tbsp honey
- 1 cup polenta
- Grated Parmesan cheese for serving

From the enchanting vineyards of Italy comes the Balsamic Glazed Sirloin. This dish marries the succulence of sirloin with the tang of balsamic vinegar and the sweetness of honey.
Glaze sirloin with balsamic-honey mixture. Sear, then roast. Serve with creamy polenta.
Let the romance of Tuscany grace your palate!

Directions

1. Preheat oven to 400°F (200°C).
2. Mix balsamic vinegar and honey.
3. Glaze the sirloin with the mixture.
4. Sear the steak in a hot pan.
5. Transfer to the oven and roast until desired doneness.
6. Prepare polenta according to package instructions.
7. Serve the sirloin slices with creamy polenta and a sprinkle of Parmesan cheese.

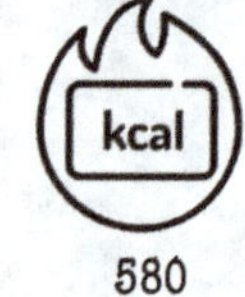

1
person

580
calories

45
minutes

Indian Saagwala Spiced Sirloin

Ingredients:

- 1 Sirloin steak
- Salt and pepper to taste
- 1/4 cup yogurt
- 1 tsp garam masala
- 1 tsp turmeric
- 1 tsp cumin
- 1 tsp coriander
- 1 tsp chili powder
- 2 cups fresh spinach, chopped
- 1/2 cup heavy cream

From the vibrant streets of India comes the Saagwala Spiced Sirloin. This dish blends the aromatic charm of Indian spices with the succulence of sirloin, all nestled in a bed of creamy spinach saag.
Marinate sirloin with spices, yogurt. Grill and serve over saag.
Embark on a flavorful journey across the subcontinent!

Directions

1. In a bowl, mix yogurt, garam masala, turmeric, cumin, coriander, chili powder, salt, and pepper.
2. Marinate the sirloin for 30 minutes.
3. Grill the steak until done to your liking.
4. In a separate pan, sauté chopped spinach until wilted.
5. Blend spinach with heavy cream to create saag.
6. Serve the sirloin over a bed of creamy saag.

1
person

550
calories

20
minutes

Greek Lemon-Oregano Sirloin

Ingredients:

- 1 Sirloin steak
- Salt and pepper to taste
- Juice of 1 lemon
- 2 tbsp fresh oregano, chopped
- 3 cloves garlic, minced
- Greek salad for serving

From the idyllic islands of Greece comes the Lemon-Oregano Sirloin. This dish captures the essence of the Mediterranean with the freshness of lemon and the earthiness of oregano.
Marinate sirloin with lemon, oregano, garlic. Grill to perfection. Serve with Greek salad.
Let the azure waves of Greece wash over your palate!

Directions

1. Mix lemon juice, oregano, garlic, salt, and pepper.
2. Marinate the sirloin for 15 minutes.
3. Grill the steak until nicely charred and cooked.
4. Serve the sirloin with a refreshing Greek salad.

1
person

530
calories

30
minutes

Japanese Teriyaki Sirloin

Ingredients:

- 1 Sirloin steak
- Salt and pepper to taste
- 1/4 cup soy sauce
- 2 tbsp mirin
- 2 tbsp sake
- 1 tbsp sugar
- Steamed rice and steamed vegetables
for serving

Inspired by the Land of the Rising Sun, the
Teriyaki Sirloin offers a blend of sweet and savory
Japanese flavors. With a teriyaki glaze, this dish
pays homage to the art of Japanese grilling.
Glaze sirloin with teriyaki sauce. Sear, then serve
with steamed rice and vegetables.
Embark on a culinary journey to Japan!

Directions

1. In a bowl, mix soy sauce, mirin, sake,
and sugar.
2. Glaze the sirloin with the teriyaki
mixture.
3. Sear the steak in a hot pan.
4. Serve the sirloin slices over steamed
rice and vegetables.

1
person

610
calories

50
minutes

Brazilian Garlic-Butter Picanha

Ingredients:

- 1 Picanha steak
- Salt to taste
- 4 tbsp butter
- 4 cloves garlic, minced

From the vibrant streets of Brazil comes the Garlic-Butter Picanha. This dish marries the succulence of picanha with the richness of garlic butter, creating a carnivore's delight.
Season picanha with salt. Grill and serve with garlic butter.
Let the samba rhythms infuse your culinary journey!

Directions

1. Preheat the grill to medium-high heat.
2. Generously season the picanha with salt.
3. Grill the steak to your desired doneness.
4. In a pan, melt the butter and sauté minced garlic until fragrant.
5. Serve the picanha with a dollop of garlic butter.

2
skewers

480
calories

40
minutes

Korean Bulgogi Sirloin Skewers

Ingredients:

- 1 Sirloin steak, cubed
- Salt and pepper to taste
- 1/4 cup soy sauce
- 2 tbsp brown sugar
- 2 cloves garlic, minced
- 1 tbsp grated ginger
- Cooked rice and kimchi for serving

Straight from the vibrant streets of Seoul, the Bulgogi Sirloin Skewers offer a blend of sweet and savory Korean flavors. Marinated in a soy-ginger mixture, these skewers are a culinary delight. Marinate sirloin in soy, ginger, garlic. Thread onto skewers, grill. Serve with rice and kimchi. Embark on a K-food adventure!

Directions

1. In a bowl, mix soy sauce, brown sugar, garlic, and ginger.
2. Marinate the sirloin cubes for 30 minutes.
3. Thread the marinated beef onto skewers.
4. Grill the skewers until nicely caramelized.
5. Serve the skewers with rice and kimchi.

1
person

570
calories

55
minutes

Argentinean Churrasco de Cuadril

Ingredients:

- 1 Cuadril (bottom sirloin) steak
- Salt and pepper to taste
- Chimichurri sauce
- Assorted vegetables for grilling

From the grand pampas of Argentina, the Churrasco de Cuadril is a celebration of South American grilling mastery. This dish showcases the succulence of cuadril (bottom sirloin) with a chimichurri marinade.
Marinate cuadril in chimichurri. Grill and serve with grilled vegetables.
Let the spirit of the gauchos infuse your feast!

Directions

1. In a bowl, marinate the cuadril steak in chimichurri sauce.
2. Season the steak with salt and pepper.
3. Grill the steak until done to your liking.
4. Grill the assorted vegetables until tender.
5. Serve the cuadril steak with the grilled vegetables.

Chapter 3:
Tenderloin
Temptations

1
person

550
calories

25
minutes

French Filet Mignon au Poivre

Ingredients:

- 1 Filet Mignon steak
- Salt to taste
- 2 tbsp black peppercorns, cracked
- 2 tbsp butter
- 1/4 cup cognac
- 1/4 cup heavy cream

From the romantic bistros of Paris, the Filet Mignon au Poivre is a classic French delight. This dish harmonizes the tenderness of filet mignon with the boldness of cracked black peppercorns. Coat filet with cracked pepper. Sear, then deglaze with cognac and cream.
Let the City of Love serenade your palate!

Directions

1. Season the filet with salt and press cracked peppercorns onto both sides.
2. Heat butter in a pan and sear the steak for 3-4 minutes per side.
3. Remove the steak from the pan.
4. Add cognac to the pan and ignite to flambé.
5. Stir in cream, simmer until the sauce thickens.
6. Pour the sauce over the filet and serve.

2
tamales

520
calories

60
minutes

Mexican Tenderloin Tamales

Ingredients:

- 1/2 lb Tenderloin, shredded
- Salt and pepper to taste
- 2 cups masa harina
- 1 cup chicken broth
- Corn husks, soaked
- Salsa for serving

From the vibrant kitchens of Mexico, the Tenderloin Tamales are a celebration of tradition and flavor. This dish wraps tenderloin in a blanket of masa, steamed to perfection.
Season tenderloin, sear, and shred. Prepare masa and assemble tamales. Steam until done.
Let the mariachi rhythms guide your culinary journey!

Directions

1. Season the shredded tenderloin with salt and pepper.
2. In a bowl, mix masa harina and chicken broth to form a smooth dough.
3. Spread masa onto soaked corn husks, add shredded tenderloin.
4. Fold the husks and steam the tamales for 45-50 minutes.
5. Serve the tamales with salsa for a true Mexican fiesta!

1
person

600
calories

35
minutes

Brazilian Coffee-Rubbed Picanha

Ingredients:

- 1 Picanha steak
- Salt and pepper to taste
- 2 tbsp ground coffee
- 1 tbsp brown sugar
- 1 tsp smoked paprika
- 1/2 tsp cayenne pepper
- Farofa for serving

From the bustling streets of Brazil comes the Coffee-Rubbed Picanha. This dish marries the succulence of picanha with the aromatic allure of coffee and spices.
Rub picanha with coffee and spices. Grill to perfection. Serve with farofa.
Let the samba rhythms infuse your culinary journey!

Directions

1. Preheat the grill to medium-high heat.
2. Mix ground coffee, brown sugar, paprika, cayenne, salt, and pepper.
3. Rub the mixture onto the picanha.
4. Grill the steak to your desired doneness.
5. Serve the picanha with a side of farofa for an authentic Brazilian experience.

 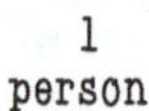  

1
person

540
calories

40
minutes

Greek Spinach and Feta-Stuffed Tenderloin

Ingredients:

- 1 Tenderloin steak, butterflied
- Salt and pepper to taste
- 2 cups fresh spinach, chopped
- 1/2 cup crumbled feta cheese
- 2 lemons
- 4 large potatoes, peeled and quartered

From the shores of Greece, the Spinach and Feta-Stuffed Tenderloin emerges as a culinary masterpiece. This dish intertwines tenderloin with the freshness of spinach and the tang of feta cheese.
Butterfly tenderloin, stuff with spinach and feta. Roll and roast. Serve with lemon potatoes.
Let the azure waves of Greece grace your feast!

Directions

1. Preheat the oven to 400°F (200°C).
2. Season the butterflied tenderloin with salt and pepper.
3. Spread spinach and feta over the tenderloin.
4. Roll the tenderloin and tie with kitchen twine.
5. Roast the tenderloin for 25-30 minutes.
6. Toss potatoes with olive oil, lemon juice, salt, and pepper. Roast alongside the tenderloin.
7. Slice the tenderloin and serve with lemon potatoes.

1
person

530
calories

45
minutes

Japanese Yakiniku-Style Tenderloin

Ingredients:

- 1 Tenderloin steak
- Salt and pepper to taste
- 1/4 cup soy sauce
- 2 cloves garlic, minced
- 1 tsp grated ginger
- Steamed rice for serving

Inspired by the bustling streets of Tokyo, the Yakiniku-Style Tenderloin offers a symphony of Japanese flavors. Marinated in a soy-garlic mixture, this dish captures the essence of Japanese grilling.
Marinate tenderloin in soy, garlic, ginger. Grill and serve with steamed rice.
Embark on a culinary journey to Japan!

Directions

1. In a bowl, mix soy sauce, garlic, and ginger.
2. Marinate the tenderloin for 30 minutes.
3. Grill the steak to your liking.
4. Let it rest before slicing.
5. Serve the tenderloin over steamed rice for an authentic Japanese experience.

1
person

520
calories

50
minutes

Turkish Pide with Tenderloin

Ingredients:

- 1 Tenderloin steak, sliced
- Salt and pepper to taste
- Pide dough
- 1 cup plain yogurt
- Fresh mint leaves for garnish

From the bustling markets of Istanbul comes the Pide with Tenderloin. This Turkish delight unites tenderloin with the charm of pide, a boat-shaped flatbread.
Sear tenderloin, prepare pide dough. Assemble and bake. Serve with yogurt sauce.
Let the Bosphorus breeze inspire your culinary adventure!

Directions

1. Sear the sliced tenderloin until nicely browned.
2. Preheat the oven to 400°F (200°C).
3. Roll out the pide dough and shape into boat-like forms.
4. Arrange the cooked tenderloin slices on the pide dough.
5. Bake the pide in the oven until golden.
6. Mix yogurt with salt and pepper.
7. Serve the tenderloin pide with a dollop of yogurt sauce and fresh mint leaves.

1
person

610
calories

30
minutes

Italian Porcini-Crusted T-Bone

Ingredients:

- 1 T-Bone steak
- Salt and pepper to taste
- 1/2 cup dried porcini mushrooms, ground
- 2 tbsp olive oil
- 2 large potatoes, peeled and diced
- Truffle oil for drizzling

From the rustic kitchens of Italy, the Porcini-Crusted T-Bone is a flavorful symphony. This dish marries the succulence of T-bone with the earthiness of porcini mushrooms.
Coat T-bone with porcini crust. Grill to perfection. Serve with truffle mashed potatoes.
Let the Italian countryside fill your plate!

Directions

1. Preheat the grill to high heat.
2. Season the T-bone with salt and pepper.
3. Coat the T-bone with the ground porcini mushrooms.
4. Grill the steak to your desired doneness.
5. Boil and mash the potatoes, drizzle with truffle oil.
6. Serve the T-bone with truffle mashed potatoes for a true taste of Italy!

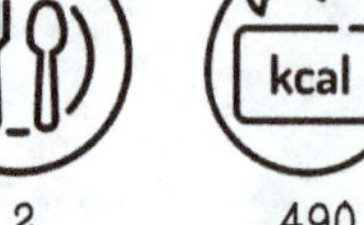

2
skewers

490
calories

55
minutes

Indian Tandoori Tenderloin Skewers

Ingredients:

- 1/2 lb Tenderloin, cubed
- Salt and pepper to taste
- 1/2 cup plain yogurt
- 1 tbsp tandoori spice blend
- Naan and raita for serving

Inspired by the vibrant streets of India, the Tandoori Tenderloin Skewers offer a burst of Indian flavors. Marinated in yogurt and spices, these skewers pay homage to the art of tandoori grilling.
Marinate tenderloin, thread onto skewers, grill.
Serve with naan and raita.
Embark on a culinary journey to India!

Directions

1. In a bowl, mix yogurt, tandoori spice blend, salt, and pepper.
2. Marinate the cubed tenderloin for 30 minutes.
3. Thread the marinated beef onto skewers.
4. Grill the skewers until nicely charred.
5. Serve the skewers with naan and a side of raita for an authentic Indian experience.

1
person

580
calories

40
minutes

Korean Grilled Tenderloin with Gochujang

Ingredients:

- 1 Tenderloin steak
- Salt and pepper to taste
- 1/4 cup gochujang
- 2 tbsp soy sauce
- 2 tbsp brown sugar
- Kimchi and rice for serving

Straight from the vibrant streets of Seoul, the Grilled Tenderloin with Gochujang offers a harmony of Korean flavors. Marinated in a spicy-sweet gochujang mixture, this dish dances across the palate.
Marinate tenderloin in gochujang and soy. Grill and serve with kimchi and rice.
Embark on a K-food adventure!

Directions

1. In a bowl, mix gochujang, soy sauce, brown sugar, salt, and pepper.
2. Marinate the tenderloin for 30 minutes.
3. Grill the steak until caramelized.
4. Serve the tenderloin with a side of kimchi and rice for a true taste of Korea!

 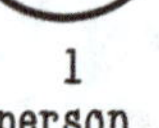  

1
person

550
calories

30
minutes

Argentinean Grilled Tenderloin Medallions

Ingredients:

- Tenderloin medallions
- Salt and pepper to taste
- Olive oil for brushing
- Chimichurri sauce for serving

From the vast pampas of Argentina, the Grilled Tenderloin Medallions are a tribute to Argentine grilling tradition. This dish showcases tenderloin medallions with a simple marinade and expert grilling.
Marinate medallions, grill to perfection. Serve with chimichurri.
Let the spirit of the gauchos infuse your feast!

Directions

1. Season the tenderloin medallions with salt and pepper.
2. Brush with olive oil.
3. Grill the medallions until done to your liking.
4. Serve the medallions with a generous drizzle of chimichurri sauce for an authentic Argentine experience.

Chapter 4:
Flank and Skirt Wonders

 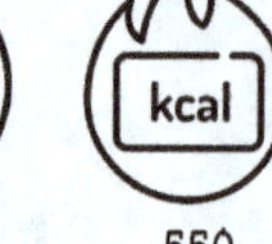 

1
person

550
calories

35
minutes

Moroccan Spiced Flank Fusion

Ingredients:

- 1 Flank steak
- Salt and pepper to taste
- 1 tsp cumin
- 1 tsp paprika
- 1/2 tsp cinnamon
- 1/2 tsp coriander
- Couscous and harissa for serving

From the bustling medinas of Morocco, the Spiced Flank Fusion is a tapestry of North African flavors. This dish melds the tenderness of flank steak with the warmth of Moroccan spices.
Rub flank steak with spices. Sear, then serve with couscous and harissa.
Let the desert winds guide your culinary adventure!

Directions

1. Preheat the grill to medium-high heat.
2. Mix cumin, paprika, cinnamon, coriander, salt, and pepper.
3. Rub the mixture onto the flank steak.
4. Sear the steak for 3-4 minutes per side.
5. Let it rest before slicing.
6. Serve the flank steak over couscous with a dollop of harissa for an authentic Moroccan experience.

1
person

530
calories

30
minutes

Greek Lemon-Oregano Skirt Steak

Ingredients:

- 1 Skirt steak
- Salt and pepper to taste
- Juice of 1 lemon
- 2 tbsp fresh oregano, chopped
- 3 cloves garlic, minced
- Greek salad for serving

From the idyllic islands of Greece comes the Lemon-Oregano Skirt Steak. This dish captures the essence of the Mediterranean with the freshness of lemon and the earthiness of oregano.
Marinate skirt steak with lemon, oregano, garlic. Grill to perfection. Serve with Greek salad.
Let the azure waves of Greece wash over your palate!

Directions

1. Mix lemon juice, oregano, garlic, salt, and pepper.
2. Marinate the skirt steak for 15 minutes.
3. Grill the steak until nicely charred and cooked.
4. Serve the skirt steak with a refreshing Greek salad.

2 tacos

490
calories

40
minutes

Mexican Skirt Steak Tacos with Mango Salsa

Ingredients:

- 1 Skirt steak, sliced
- Salt and pepper to taste
- 2 tbsp lime juice
- 2 tbsp olive oil
- 1 tsp chili powder
- 1/2 tsp cumin
- Flour tortillas
- Mango salsa for serving

Inspired by the vibrant streets of Mexico, the Skirt Steak Tacos with Mango Salsa are a fiesta of colors and flavors. Marinated skirt steak meets the sweetness of mango salsa in a tortilla embrace. Marinate skirt steak, grill, and serve in tortillas with mango salsa.
Let the Mariachi tunes accompany your culinary journey!

Directions

1. In a bowl, mix lime juice, olive oil, chili powder, cumin, salt, and pepper.
2. Marinate the sliced skirt steak for 20 minutes.
3. Grill the steak until nicely charred.
4. Warm the flour tortillas.
5. Serve the skirt steak in tortillas with a generous scoop of mango salsa.

1
person

600
calories

35
minutes

Brazilian Garlic-Butter Picanha

Ingredients:

- 1 Picanha steak
- Salt to taste
- 4 tbsp butter
- 4 cloves garlic, minced

From the vibrant streets of Brazil comes the Garlic-Butter Picanha. This dish marries the succulence of picanha with the richness of garlic butter, creating a carnivore's delight.
Season picanha with salt. Grill and serve with garlic butter.
Let the samba rhythms infuse your culinary journey!

Directions

1. Preheat the grill to medium-high heat.
2. Generously season the picanha with salt.
3. Grill the steak to your desired doneness.
4. In a pan, melt the butter and sauté minced garlic until fragrant.
5. Serve the picanha with a dollop of garlic butter.

1
person

520
calories

30
minutes

Italian Grilled Balsamic Flank Steak

Ingredients:

- 1 Flank steak
- Salt and pepper to taste
- 1/4 cup balsamic vinegar
- 2 tbsp honey
- Assorted roasted vegetables for serving

From the enchanting vineyards of Italy comes the Grilled Balsamic Flank Steak. This dish marries the succulence of flank steak with the tang of balsamic vinegar and the sweetness of honey. Marinate flank steak with balsamic-honey mixture. Grill and serve with roasted vegetables. Let the romance of Tuscany grace your palate!

Directions

1. Preheat the grill to medium-high heat.
2. Mix balsamic vinegar and honey.
3. Marinate the flank steak with the mixture.
4. Grill the steak to your desired doneness.
5. Let it rest before slicing.
6. Serve the flank steak with a side of assorted roasted vegetables for an authentic Italian experience.

1
person

540
calories

45
minutes

Indian Spiced Flank Steak with Raita

Ingredients:

- 1 Flank steak
- Salt and pepper to taste
- 2 tsp garam masala
- 1 tsp cumin
- 1/2 tsp turmeric
- 1/2 tsp chili powder
- 1/2 cup plain yogurt
- Raita and naan for serving

Inspired by the vibrant bazaars of India, the Spiced Flank Steak with Raita offers a dance of spices and cooling yogurt. Marinated flank steak meets the refreshing tang of raita.
Marinate flank steak, grill, and serve with raita and naan.
Embark on a spice-infused culinary journey to India!

Directions

1. Preheat the grill to medium-high heat.
2. Mix garam masala, cumin, turmeric, chili powder, salt, and pepper.
3. Rub the mixture onto the flank steak.
4. Marinate the steak for 30 minutes.
5. Grill the steak to your liking.
6. Mix yogurt, salt, and pepper to make raita.
7. Serve the flank steak with raita and naan for a true taste of India!

2 wraps

510
calories

50
minutes

Korean Bulgogi Skirt Steak Wraps

Ingredients:

- 1 Skirt steak, sliced
- Salt and pepper to taste
- 1/4 cup soy sauce
- 2 tbsp brown sugar
- 1 tbsp sesame oil
- 2 cloves garlic, minced
- Lettuce leaves for wrapping

Straight from the bustling streets of Seoul, the Bulgogi Skirt Steak Wraps offer a blend of sweet and savory Korean flavors. Marinated in a soy-sesame mixture, these wraps are a handheld delight.
Marinate skirt steak, grill, and wrap in lettuce leaves.
Embark on a K-food adventure!

Directions

1. In a bowl, mix soy sauce, brown sugar, sesame oil, garlic, salt, and pepper.
2. Marinate the sliced skirt steak for 30 minutes.
3. Grill the steak until caramelized.
4. Arrange the cooked steak on lettuce leaves.
5. Roll up the leaves to make wraps.
6. Serve the wraps for an authentic Korean experience!

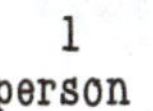

1
person

530
calories

40
minutes

Japanese Ginger-Soy Sirloin

Ingredients:

- 1 Sirloin steak
- Salt and pepper to taste
- 2 tbsp soy sauce
- 1 tbsp sake
- 1 tbsp grated ginger
- Steamed rice for serving

Inspired by the Land of the Rising Sun, the Ginger-Soy Sirloin offers a fusion of Japanese flavors. Marinated in a ginger-soy mixture, this dish pays homage to the art of Japanese grilling. Marinate sirloin in ginger, soy, and sake. Grill and serve with steamed rice.
Embark on a culinary journey to Japan!

Directions

1. In a bowl, mix soy sauce, sake, grated ginger, salt, and pepper.
2. Marinate the sirloin for 30 minutes.
3. Grill the steak to your liking.
4. Let it rest before slicing.
5. Serve the sirloin over steamed rice for a true taste of Japan!

2
skewers

500
calories

55
minutes

Turkish Grilled Adana Kebabs

Ingredients:

- 1/2 lb ground meat (beef or lamb)
- Salt and pepper to taste
- 1 tsp paprika
- 1/2 tsp cumin
- 1/2 tsp sumac
- Pide and yogurt sauce for serving

From the vibrant bazaars of Istanbul comes the Grilled Adana Kebabs. This Turkish delight offers a blend of spiced ground meat, grilled to perfection on skewers.
Prepare Adana mixture, thread onto skewers, and grill. Serve with pide and yogurt sauce.
Let the Bosphorus breeze inspire your feast!

Directions

1. Preheat the grill to medium-high heat.
2. Mix ground meat, paprika, cumin, sumac, salt, and pepper.
3. Shape the mixture onto skewers.
4. Grill the kebabs until nicely charred.
5. Warm the pide.
6. Serve the kebabs with pide and a side of yogurt sauce for an authentic Turkish experience.

1
person

570
calories

45
minutes

Argentinean Flank Steak Roll-Ups

Ingredients:

- 1 Flank steak
- Salt and pepper to taste
- Assorted vegetables for filling
- Shredded cheese for filling
- Chimichurri sauce for serving

From the grand pampas of Argentina, the Flank Steak Roll-Ups are a celebration of South American grilling mastery. This dish showcases the versatility of flank steak with a delightful filling. Roll up flank steak with vegetables and cheese. Grill and serve with chimichurri. Let the spirit of the gauchos infuse your feast!

Directions

1. Preheat the grill to medium-high heat.
2. Season the flank steak with salt and pepper.
3. Arrange the assorted vegetables and shredded cheese over the steak.
4. Roll up the steak and secure with toothpicks.
5. Grill the roll-ups until cooked and cheese is melted.
6. Serve the roll-ups with a drizzle of chimichurri sauce for an authentic Argentine experience.

Chapter 5:
Specialty Cuts
Showcase

1
person

580
calories

50
minutes

Thai Pineapple Beef Curry with Flat Iron

Ingredients:

- 1 Flat Iron steak
- Salt and pepper to taste
- 1 can coconut milk
- 2 tbsp red curry paste
- 1 cup fresh pineapple chunks
- Fresh cilantro for garnish
- Jasmine rice for serving

From the bustling markets of Thailand, the Pineapple Beef Curry with Flat Iron is a harmonious blend of sweet, spicy, and savory flavors. This dish marries flat iron steak with the vibrant essence of Thai curry.
Cook flat iron, prepare curry, and serve with jasmine rice.
Embark on a Thai culinary adventure!

Directions

1. Preheat the grill to medium-high heat.
2. Season the flat iron steak with salt and pepper.
3. Grill the steak to your liking.
4. In a pan, simmer coconut milk and red curry paste.
5. Add pineapple chunks and cooked flat iron.
6. Serve the curry over jasmine rice, garnished with fresh cilantro.

2
enchilad
as

560
calories

60
minutes

Mexican Ribeye Enchiladas

Ingredients:

- 1 Ribeye steak, cooked and shredded
- Salt and pepper to taste
- Corn tortillas
- 2 cups enchilada sauce
- 1 cup shredded cheese
- Sour cream and chopped green onions for serving

Straight from the heart of Mexico, the Ribeye Enchiladas are a celebration of rich flavors and comforting textures. This dish wraps ribeye in corn tortillas, smothered in a flavorful enchilada sauce.
Cook ribeye, prepare sauce, assemble enchiladas, and bake.
Let the mariachi melodies serenade your palate!

Directions

1. Preheat the oven to 375°F (190°C).
2. Season the shredded ribeye with salt and pepper.
3. Warm the corn tortillas.
4. Fill each tortilla with shredded ribeye, roll up, and place in a baking dish.
5. Pour enchilada sauce over the rolled tortillas.
6. Sprinkle shredded cheese over the top.
7. Bake in the oven until cheese is melted and bubbly.
8. Serve the enchiladas with a dollop of sour cream and a sprinkle of chopped green onions.

1
person

540
calories

40
minutes

Greek Beef Souvlaki with Hanger Steak

Ingredients:

- 1 Hanger steak
- Salt and pepper to taste
- 2 tbsp olive oil
- Juice of 1 lemon
- 2 cloves garlic, minced
- Pita bread and tzatziki for serving

From the sun-kissed islands of Greece, the Beef Souvlaki with Hanger Steak offers a taste of the Mediterranean breeze. This dish threads hanger steak onto skewers and grills it to perfection. Marinate hanger steak, thread onto skewers, and serve with pita and tzatziki.
Let the azure waves of Greece inspire your feast!

Directions

1. Preheat the grill to medium-high heat.
2. Mix olive oil, lemon juice, garlic, salt, and pepper.
3. Marinate the hanger steak for 30 minutes.
4. Thread the steak onto skewers.
5. Grill the skewers until nicely charred and cooked.
6. Warm the pita bread.
7. Serve the skewers with pita bread and a side of tzatziki for an authentic Greek experience.

1
person

620
calories

35
minutes

Italian Gorgonzola-Stuffed Ribeye

Ingredients:

- 1 Ribeye steak
- Salt and pepper to taste
- 1/4 cup gorgonzola cheese, crumbled
- 2 tbsp butter
- 2 cloves garlic, minced
- Roasted potatoes for serving

From the rolling hills of Italy, the Gorgonzola-Stuffed Ribeye is a symphony of robust flavors. This dish stuffs ribeye with creamy gorgonzola cheese and grills it to perfection.
Prepare ribeye, stuff with cheese, and grill. Serve with roasted potatoes.
Let the romance of Tuscany grace your plate!

Directions

1. Preheat the grill to medium-high heat.
2. Season the ribeye with salt and pepper.
3. Make a slit in the steak and stuff with gorgonzola cheese.
4. In a pan, melt butter and sauté minced garlic.
5. Grill the steak until cooked to your liking.
6. Serve the ribeye with a drizzle of garlic butter and a side of roasted potatoes for an authentic Italian experience.

1
person

530
calories

45
minutes

Japanese Hibachi-Style Sirloin

Ingredients:

- 1 Sirloin steak
- Salt and pepper to taste
- 2 tbsp soy sauce
- 1 tbsp sake
- 1 tbsp mirin
- 2 tbsp vegetable oil
- Assorted vegetables for grilling
- Fried rice for serving

Inspired by the hibachi grills of Japan, the Hibachi-Style Sirloin offers a theatrical and flavorful experience. This dish marinates sirloin and grills it with vegetables.
Marinate sirloin, grill with vegetables, and serve with fried rice.
Embark on a culinary journey to Japan!

Directions

1. Preheat the grill to high heat.
2. Mix soy sauce, sake, mirin, salt, and pepper.
3. Marinate the sirloin for 30 minutes.
4. Grill the steak and vegetables until nicely charred.
5. Slice the steak.
6. Serve the grilled steak and vegetables over a bed of fried rice for an authentic hibachi experience.

 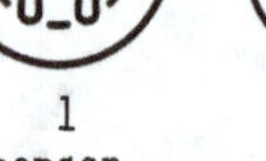  

1
person

550
calories

50
minutes

Korean Dakgalbi-Style Flank Steak

Ingredients:

- 1 Flank steak
- Salt and pepper to taste
- 1/4 cup gochujang
- 2 tbsp soy sauce
- 2 tbsp brown sugar
- 1 tbsp sesame oil
- Assorted vegetables for grilling
- Steamed rice for serving

Substitutions

-

Straight from the vibrant streets of Seoul, the Dakgalbi-Style Flank Steak offers a fusion of Korean flavors. This dish marinates flank steak in a spicy-sweet sauce and grills it to perfection. Marinate flank steak, grill, and serve with steamed rice.
Embark on a K-food adventure!

Directions

1. Preheat the grill to medium-high heat.
2. Mix gochujang, soy sauce, brown sugar, sesame oil, salt, and pepper.
3. Marinate the flank steak for 30 minutes.
4. Grill the steak and vegetables until nicely charred.
5. Serve the steak and vegetables over steamed rice for a true taste of Korea!

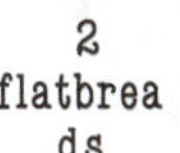

2
flatbrea
ds

520
calories

40
minutes

Turkish Lahmacun Beef Flatbreads

Ingredients:

- 1/2 lb ground beef
- Salt and pepper to taste
- 2 tbsp tomato paste
- 1 tsp ground cumin
- 1/2 tsp paprika
- Flatbread dough
- Chopped fresh parsley and lemon wedges for serving

From the bustling markets of Istanbul, the Lahmacun Beef Flatbreads offer a delectable street food experience. This dish tops flatbreads with spiced ground beef and bakes them to perfection. Prepare beef mixture, spread on flatbreads, and bake.

Embark on a Turkish culinary adventure!

Directions

1. Preheat the oven to 450°F (230°C).
2. Mix ground beef, tomato paste, cumin, paprika, salt, and pepper.
3. Roll out the flatbread dough and spread the beef mixture evenly.
4. Bake the flatbreads in the oven until the edges are golden.
5. Sprinkle chopped parsley and serve with lemon wedges.

1
person

590
calories

45
minutes

Argentinean Flank Steak with Chimichurri Potatoes

Ingredients:

- 1 Flank steak
- Salt and pepper to taste
- Potatoes, cubed
- Olive oil for roasting
- Chimichurri sauce for serving

From the vast pampas of Argentina, the Flank Steak with Chimichurri Potatoes is a tribute to Argentine grilling mastery. This dish pairs flank steak with zesty chimichurri and roasted potatoes. Cook flank steak, prepare chimichurri, roast potatoes, and serve.
Let the spirit of the gauchos infuse your feast!

Directions

1. Preheat the grill to medium-high heat.
2. Season the flank steak with salt and pepper.
3. Grill the steak to your liking.
4. Toss cubed potatoes with olive oil, salt, and pepper.
5. Roast the potatoes in the oven until golden and crispy.
6. Serve the flank steak with a generous drizzle of chimichurri sauce and a side of roasted potatoes for an authentic Argentine experience.

  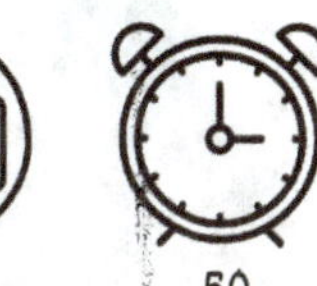

1
person

570
calories

50
minutes

Indian Beef Keema Naan Wraps

Ingredients:

- 1/2 lb ground beef
- Salt and pepper to taste
- 1 tsp garam masala
- 1/2 tsp turmeric
- 1/2 tsp cumin
- Naan bread
- Chopped fresh cilantro and yogurt for serving

Inspired by the vibrant bazaars of India, the Beef Keema Naan Wraps offer a burst of Indian flavors. This dish sautés spiced ground beef and serves it in warm naan bread.
Prepare beef keema, warm naan, and assemble wraps.
Embark on a spice-infused culinary journey to India!

Directions

1. In a pan, sauté ground beef until browned.
2. Season the beef with salt, pepper, garam masala, turmeric, and cumin.
3. Warm the naan bread.
4. Spoon the beef keema onto the naan.
5. Garnish with chopped cilantro and a dollop of yogurt.
6. Fold the naan to make wraps.
7. Serve the wraps for an authentic Indian experience!

1
person

630
calories

40
minutes

Brazilian Bacon-Wrapped Ribeye

Ingredients:

- 1 Ribeye steak
- Salt and pepper to taste
- Bacon slices
- Farofa and Brazilian salsa for serving

From the sizzling churrasco grills of Brazil, the Bacon-Wrapped Ribeye is a carnivore's dream come true. This dish wraps ribeye in smoky bacon and grills it to perfection.
Wrap ribeye with bacon, grill, and serve with farofa and Brazilian salsa.
Let the samba rhythms infuse your feast!

Directions

1. Preheat the grill to medium-high heat.
2. Season the ribeye with salt and pepper.
3. Wrap the ribeye with bacon slices.
4. Grill the steak until cooked to your liking.
5. Serve the ribeye with a side of farofa and a generous spoonful of Brazilian salsa for an authentic churrasco experience.

Asking for support

Hey there, fellow flavor adventurers! While we're savoring these recipes, let's take a moment for something special – a chance for you to make a real impact.

Reviews, my friends, are like gold dust to us. If a recipe has sparked your culinary joy, could you spare a quick moment to share your thoughts?

You know the drill – that review button is where the magic happens. A star rating and a sentence – it's a small gesture with a big ripple effect.

Why do reviews matter? Well, we're not backed by megaphone marketing. We're a small crew with a big passion, and your reviews? They're the wind in our sails, helping us navigate the vast sea of publishing.

Your words are read with gratitude and excitement. Imagine us, huddled around screens, soaking in your insights like a warm kitchen aroma.

Now, about the occasional hiccup – we're human, riding the rollercoaster of creativity. I hope you'll overlook these quirks and focus on the heart in each recipe.

But let's steer back to the main course: the recipes. The world of steaks, the sizzle, the adventure on your plate. Your review, whether written or not, makes you part of this journey, and for that, I'm grateful.

So, as we explore these dishes, keep that review in mind. Your presence here fuels our passion. Now, let's dive back into the recipes and create culinary magic together.

Chapter 6:
Global Steak
Creations

1
person

590
calories

50
minutes

South African Braai Ribeye

Ingredients:

- 1 Ribeye steak
- Salt and pepper to taste
- 2 tbsp paprika
- 1 tbsp ground coriander
- 1 tsp ground cumin
- 1 tsp garlic powder
- Chakalaka for serving

Straight from the South African savannas, the Braai Ribeye celebrates the art of open-fire grilling. This dish marinates ribeye in a bold spice rub and sears it over open flames.
Marinate ribeye, braai over open flames, and serve with chakalaka.
Let the wild beauty of Africa ignite your feast!

Directions

1. Preheat the braai (open-fire grill) to medium-high heat.
2. Mix paprika, coriander, cumin, garlic powder, salt, and pepper.
3. Season the ribeye with the spice rub.
4. Grill the ribeye over open flames until charred and cooked to your liking.
5. Serve the ribeye with a side of chakalaka for an authentic South African experience.

2 tacos

550
calories

45
minutes

Mexican Carne Asada Tacos

Ingredients:

- 1 Skirt steak
- Salt and pepper to taste
- Juice of 2 limes
- Juice of 1 orange
- 2 cloves garlic, minced
- Corn tortillas
- Salsa and chopped cilantro for serving

From the lively streets of Mexico, the Carne Asada Tacos are a fiesta of flavors. This dish marinates thinly sliced steak in zesty citrus and grills it to perfection.
Marinate steak, grill, and serve in tortillas with salsa.
Let the mariachi melodies serenade your taste buds!

Directions

1. Mix lime juice, orange juice, garlic, salt, and pepper.
2. Marinate the skirt steak for 30 minutes.
3. Grill the steak until nicely charred.
4. Warm the corn tortillas.
5. Slice the steak and assemble the tacos.
6. Serve the tacos with salsa and a sprinkle of chopped cilantro for an authentic Mexican experience.

1
person

530
calories

40
minutes

Thai Lemongrass-Marinated Sirloin

Ingredients:

- 1 Sirloin steak
- Salt and pepper to taste
- 2 stalks lemongrass, minced
- 2 cloves garlic, minced
- 1 red chili, minced
- 2 tbsp fish sauce
- Sticky rice for serving

Inspired by the aromatic markets of Thailand, the Lemongrass-Marinated Sirloin is a symphony of vibrant flavors. This dish marinates sirloin in lemongrass and grills it to perfection.
Marinate sirloin, grill, and serve with sticky rice. Embark on a culinary journey to Thailand!

Directions

1. In a bowl, mix lemongrass, garlic, chili, fish sauce, salt, and pepper.
2. Marinate the sirloin for 30 minutes.
3. Grill the steak until cooked to your liking.
4. Let it rest before slicing.
5. Serve the sirloin over a bed of sticky rice for a true taste of Thailand!

1
person

600
calories

55
minutes

Italian Rosemary Ribeye Roast

Ingredients:

- 1 Ribeye steak
- Salt and pepper to taste
- 3 tbsp olive oil
- 3 sprigs fresh rosemary
- 4 cloves garlic, smashed
- Assorted vegetables for roasting

From the rustic kitchens of Italy, the Rosemary Ribeye Roast is a celebration of aromatic herbs and succulent meat. This dish roasts ribeye with fragrant rosemary and garlic.
Prepare ribeye, roast with herbs, and serve with roasted vegetables.
Let the romance of Tuscany grace your feast!

Directions

1. Preheat the oven to 375°F (190°C).
2. Season the ribeye with salt and pepper.
3. Rub the ribeye with olive oil, rosemary, and smashed garlic.
4. Roast the ribeye in the oven until cooked to your liking.
5. Meanwhile, roast the vegetables in the oven.
6. Let the ribeye rest before slicing.
7. Serve the ribeye slices with a side of roasted vegetables for an authentic Italian experience.

1
person

580
calories

60
minutes

Brazilian Feijoada with Beef

Ingredients:

- Assorted beef cuts (short ribs, sausages, etc.)
- Salt and pepper to taste
- 1 onion, chopped
- 4 cloves garlic, minced
- 2 cups black beans, cooked
- Rice and farofa for serving

From the heart of Brazil, the Feijoada with Beef is a symphony of flavors that celebrates the nation's culinary heritage. This dish combines various cuts of beef in a hearty bean stew.
Prepare beef cuts, simmer with beans, and serve with rice and farofa.
Let the rhythms of samba elevate your feast!

Directions

1. Season the assorted beef cuts with salt and pepper.
2. In a pot, sauté onion and garlic until fragrant.
3. Add the beef cuts and brown on all sides.
4. Add the cooked black beans and simmer until flavors meld.
5. Prepare rice and farofa for serving.
6. Serve the feijoada with a side of rice and a sprinkle of farofa for an authentic Brazilian experience.

1
person

540
calories

45
minutes

Greek Gyro-Inspired Sirloin

Ingredients:

- 1 Sirloin steak
- Salt and pepper to taste
- 1 tsp dried oregano
- 1 tsp dried thyme
- 1 tsp garlic powder
- Pita bread and tzatziki for serving

Inspired by the Mediterranean breeze, the Gyro-Inspired Sirloin is a delightful fusion of flavors. This dish marinates sirloin with Greek-inspired spices and grills it to perfection.
Marinate sirloin, grill, and serve in pita with tzatziki.
Embark on a journey to the Greek Isles!

Directions

1. Mix dried oregano, dried thyme, garlic powder, salt, and pepper.
2. Season the sirloin with the spice mix.
3. Grill the steak until cooked to your liking.
4. Let the steak rest before slicing.
5. Warm the pita bread.
6. Serve the sliced sirloin in pita bread with a generous dollop of tzatziki for an authentic Greek experience.

1
person

520
calories

50
minutes

Japanese Miso-Marinated Sirloin

Ingredients:

- 1 Sirloin steak
- Salt and pepper to taste
- 2 tbsp white miso paste
- 1 tbsp soy sauce
- 1 tbsp mirin
- 1 tbsp sake
- Steamed rice for serving

Inspired by the umami-rich cuisine of Japan, the Miso-Marinated Sirloin is a symphony of flavors. This dish marinates sirloin in a savory miso mixture and grills it to perfection.
Marinate sirloin, grill, and serve with steamed rice.
Embark on a culinary journey to Japan!

Directions

1. Mix white miso paste, soy sauce, mirin, sake, salt, and pepper.
2. Marinate the sirloin for 30 minutes.
3. Grill the steak until nicely charred.
4. Let the steak rest before slicing.
5. Serve the sliced sirloin over a bed of steamed rice for an authentic Japanese experience.

1
person

530
calories

40
minutes

Turkish Beef Kofta Pita Pockets

Ingredients:

- 1/2 lb ground beef
- Salt and pepper to taste
- 1 tsp ground cumin
- 1 tsp ground coriander
- 1/2 tsp paprika
- Pita bread and yogurt sauce for serving

From the bustling bazaars of Istanbul, the Beef Kofta Pita Pockets offer a delectable street food experience. This dish grills spiced beef kofta and serves it in warm pita bread.
Prepare beef kofta, grill, and serve in pita with yogurt sauce.
Embark on a culinary journey to Turkey!

Directions

1. Mix ground beef, cumin, coriander, paprika, salt, and pepper.
2. Shape the beef mixture into kofta (kebab) shapes.
3. Grill the kofta until cooked through.
4. Warm the pita bread.
5. Serve the kofta in pita bread with a drizzle of yogurt sauce for an authentic Turkish experience.

1
person

560
calories

50
minutes

Indian Rogan Josh Skirt Steak

Ingredients:

- 1 Skirt steak
- Salt and pepper to taste
- 1 onion, chopped
- 2 cloves garlic, minced
- 1 tsp ground ginger
- 1 tsp ground cumin
- 1 tsp ground coriander
- 1/2 tsp turmeric
- Naan or rice for serving

Straight from the vibrant streets of India, the Rogan Josh Skirt Steak is a fusion of bold spices and tender meat. This dish simmers skirt steak in a rich and aromatic curry sauce.
Prepare curry sauce, simmer skirt steak, and serve with naan or rice.
Embark on a spice-infused culinary journey!

Directions

1. Season the skirt steak with salt and pepper.
2. In a pan, sauté onion and garlic until fragrant.
3. Add ground ginger, cumin, coriander, turmeric, salt, and pepper.
4. Add the skirt steak and brown on both sides.
5. Add water and simmer until the steak is tender.
6. Serve the skirt steak with naan or rice for an authentic Indian experience.

1
person

550
calories

45
minutes

Korean Bulgogi Ribeye Bites

Ingredients:

- 1 Ribeye steak
- Salt and pepper to taste
- 2 tbsp soy sauce
- 1 tbsp sesame oil
- 1 tbsp brown sugar
- 2 cloves garlic, minced
- Assorted vegetables for grilling

Inspired by the vibrant flavors of Korea, the Bulgogi Ribeye Bites are a delightful fusion of sweet and savory. This dish marinates ribeye in a soy-sesame marinade and grills it to perfection. Marinate ribeye, grill, and serve as bite-sized pieces.
Embark on a K-food adventure!

Directions

1. Mix soy sauce, sesame oil, brown sugar, garlic, salt, and pepper.
2. Marinate the ribeye for 30 minutes.
3. Grill the steak until nicely charred.
4. Slice the ribeye into bite-sized pieces.
5. Serve the bulgogi ribeye bites with assorted grilled vegetables for an authentic Korean experience.

Chapter 7:
Fusion Flavors and Fusions

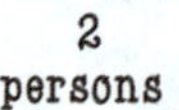

2
persons

450/ser
ving

30
minutes

Argentinean Matambre a la Pizza

Ingredients:

- 2 matambre steaks
- 1 cup pizza sauce
- 1 ½ cups shredded mozzarella
- ½ red onion, thinly sliced
- ½ red bell pepper, sliced
- 1 tsp dried oregano
- Salt and pepper, to taste
- Olive oil for drizzling

The tango of flavors in this dish tells a story of Argentinean passion and Italian zest. Legend has it, gauchos transformed pizza with a sizzling steak twist. A dance of herbs, steak, and cheese under the Argentinian sun.

Directions

1. Preheat the grill.
2. Season steaks with salt, pepper, and oregano.
3. Grill steaks until medium-rare.
4. Spread pizza sauce on top.
5. Layer cheese, onion, and bell pepper.
6. Grill until cheese melts.
7. Drizzle with olive oil.
8. Slice and serve.

1
person

380/ser
ving

25
minutes

French Herb-Crusted Filet Mignon

Ingredients:

- 1 filet mignon steak
- 2 tbsp Dijon mustard
- 2 tbsp fresh herbs (rosemary, thyme, parsley), chopped
- 2 cloves garlic, minced
- Salt and pepper, to taste
- Olive oil
- ½ cup breadcrumbs

In the heart of Parisian bistros, this filet mignon emerges as a culinary masterpiece. A symphony of herbs and tender beef—each bite a reminder of the Eiffel Tower's elegant embrace.

Directions

1. Preheat oven to 400°F.
2. Season steak with salt and pepper.
3. Sear in a hot pan with olive oil.
4. Brush with mustard.
5. Mix herbs, garlic, breadcrumbs, and olive oil.
6. Pack mixture on top.
7. Roast in oven for 10 mins.
8. Rest before slicing.

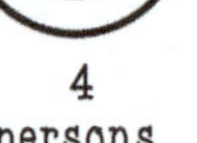

4
persons

320/ser ving

20 minutes

Mexican Steak Fajitas

Ingredients:

- 1 lb flank steak
- 2 bell peppers, sliced
- 1 onion, sliced
- 2 tbsp fajita seasoning
- Flour tortillas
- Sour cream, salsa, guacamole for serving

A sizzle and a burst of colors—the fajitas tell of Mexican streets bustling with vibrant spices. A joyful parade of steak, peppers, and onions wrapped in tortillas.

Directions

1. Marinate steak in fajita seasoning.
2. Sear on a hot skillet.
3. Remove and rest.
4. Sauté peppers and onions.
5. Slice steak against the grain.
6. Warm tortillas.
7. Assemble fajitas.
8. Serve with sides.

 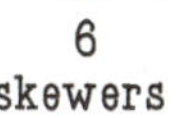  

6
skewers

280/ser
ving

35
minutes

Thai Red Curry Beef Skewers

Ingredients:

- 1 lb beef sirloin, cubed
- ¼ cup red curry paste
- ½ cup coconut milk
- 1 tbsp fish sauce
- 1 tbsp brown sugar
- Bamboo skewers, soaked
- Lime wedges for serving

From the bustling streets of Bangkok to your plate —these skewers bring the spice of Thailand to life. The melody of red curry, beef, and coconut dances on your taste buds.

Directions

1. Mix red curry paste, coconut milk, fish sauce, and sugar.
2. Marinate beef for 20 mins.
3. Thread beef onto skewers.
4. Grill until charred.
5. Serve with lime wedges.

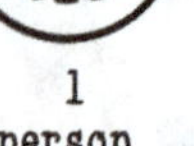

1
person

420/ser
ving

40
minutes

Italian Truffle-Infused Ribeye

Ingredients:

- 1 ribeye steak
- 2 tbsp truffle oil
- Salt and pepper, to taste
- 3 cloves garlic, minced
- 2 sprigs fresh rosemary
- 1 tbsp butter
- 1 tbsp olive oil

A voyage to Italy's culinary heart—the truffle-infused ribeye is a poem of indulgence. Each bite whispers tales of ancient olive groves and the captivating aroma of truffles.

Directions

1. Rub steak with truffle oil, salt, and pepper.
2. Sear in a hot pan.
3. Add garlic, rosemary, butter, and olive oil.
4. Baste until butter melts.
5. Rest before slicing.
6. Drizzle with extra truffle oil.

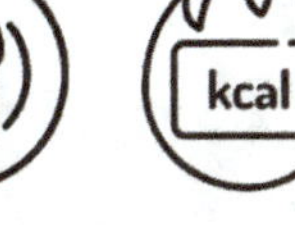

2
persons

310/ser
ving

40
minutes

Korean Kimchi-Marinated Flank Steak

Seoul's fiery spirit meets tender beef in this Korean love story. Kimchi's tang and spice embrace flank steak for a marinade that sparks a dance of flavors on your palate.

Ingredients:

- 1 lb flank steak
- ½ cup kimchi, pureed
- 2 tbsp soy sauce
- 1 tbsp sesame oil
- 2 tbsp brown sugar
- 2 green onions, chopped
- 1 tsp ginger, minced
- 1 tsp garlic, minced
- Sesame seeds for garnish

Directions

1. Mix kimchi, soy sauce, sesame oil, sugar, onions, ginger, and garlic.
2. Marinate steak for 30 mins.
3. Grill to desired doneness.
4. Rest before slicing.
5. Sprinkle sesame seeds.

 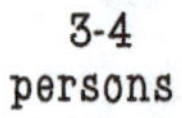  

3-4
persons

260/ser
ving

50
minutes

Turkish Beef Manti Dumplings

Ingredients:

- ½ lb ground beef
- 1 small onion, grated
- 2 cloves garlic, minced
- 1 tsp paprika
- Salt and pepper, to taste
- 1 pack dumpling wrappers
- ½ cup yogurt
- 2 tbsp butter
- Dried mint for garnish

A treasure from Turkish kitchens, manti dumplings carry tales of ancient empires. Delicate beef parcels, hugged by yogurt and kissed by mint, invite you to savor centuries of tradition.

Directions

1. Mix beef, onion, garlic, paprika, salt, and pepper.
2. Fill wrappers, fold into dumplings.
3. Boil until cooked.
4. Serve with yogurt.
5. Drizzle with melted butter.
6. Sprinkle dried mint.

 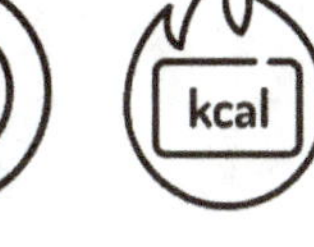 

1
person

290/ser
ving

45
minutes

Japanese Sukiyaki-Style Sirloin

Ingredients:

- 1 sirloin steak, thinly sliced
- ½ cup soy sauce
- ¼ cup mirin
- 2 tbsp sugar
- 1 onion, thinly sliced
- Assorted mushrooms
- 1 bunch bok choy
- ½ block firm tofu, cubed
- Green onions for garnish

Tokyo's bustling markets inspire this sukiyaki-style sirloin. Thin slices of beef, nestled in a sweet soy bath with vegetables and tofu—a reminder of Japan's delicate culinary artistry.

Directions

1. Mix soy sauce, mirin, and sugar for broth.
2. Arrange beef, vegetables, and tofu in a hot pot.
3. Pour broth over.
4. Simmer until cooked.
5. Serve with green onions.

1
person

360/ser
ving

35
minutes

Greek Spanakopita-Stuffed Ribeye

An ode to Greek shores—this spanakopita-stuffed ribeye is a marriage of cultures. Tender ribeye embraces the Mediterranean with spinach, feta, and a melody of herbs.

Ingredients:

- 1 ribeye steak
- 1 cup fresh spinach, sautéed
- ½ cup feta cheese, crumbled
- 2 tbsp fresh dill, chopped
- 2 tbsp fresh parsley, chopped
- Salt and pepper, to taste
- Olive oil
- Toothpicks

Directions

1. Preheat oven to 400°F.
2. Season steak.
3. Layer spinach, feta, herbs on steak.
4. Roll up and secure with toothpicks.
5. Sear in a pan with olive oil.
6. Finish in the oven.
7. Slice before serving.

4
persons

**280/ser
ving**

40
minutes

Indian Spiced Beef Keema

Ingredients:

- 1 lb ground beef
- 1 onion, chopped
- 2 cloves garlic, minced
- 1 tbsp ginger, minced
- 2 tomatoes, chopped
- 2 tsp curry powder
- 1 tsp ground cumin
- 1 cup peas
- Fresh cilantro for garnish

From the bustling markets of Mumbai, this spiced beef keema whispers tales of India's aromatic kitchens. A blend of beef, spices, and peas—a tribute to India's culinary tapestry.

Directions

1. Sauté onion, garlic, ginger.
2. Add beef, cook until browned.
3. Stir in tomatoes, spices.
4. Simmer until flavors meld.
5. Add peas, cook until tender.
6. Garnish with cilantro.
7. Serve with rice.

Chapter 8:
Steak Classics Reimagined

1
person

380
calories

15
minutes

Moroccan Mint Tea-Glazed Skirt Steak

Transport your taste buds to the bustling markets of Marrakech with this tender skirt steak, kissed by the essence of mint tea.

Ingredients:

- 1 skirt steak (8 oz)
- 1/4 cup Moroccan mint tea
- 1 tbsp olive oil
- 1 tsp paprika
- Salt and pepper to taste
- Fresh mint leaves for garnish
- Lemon wedges for serving
- Couscous for side
- Fresh vegetables for side

Directions

1. Marinate steak in mint tea, olive oil, paprika, salt, and pepper.
2. Heat grill to medium-high heat.
3. Grill steak for 3-4 minutes per side.
4. Rest, slice, and garnish with mint.
5. Serve with couscous, vegetables, and lemon wedges.
6. Bon appétit!

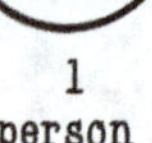

1
person

420
calories

20
minutes

Greek Beef Stifado

~~~~~~~~~~~~~~~~

Ingredients:

- 1 lb beef stew meat
- 10-12 pearl onions
- 2 cloves garlic, minced
- 1 cup red wine
- 1/4 cup balsamic vinegar
- 1 tbsp honey
- 1 cinnamon stick
- 2 bay leaves
- 1 tsp dried oregano
- Salt and pepper to taste
- Chopped fresh parsley for garnish
- Cooked rice for serving
- Crusty bread for soaking up the sauce

-

A slow-cooked dance of flavors, this Greek classic unites tender beef with aromatic spices and sweet pearl onions.

Directions

1. Sear beef until browned.
2. Add onions and garlic; sauté.
3. Pour in wine, vinegar, and honey; simmer.
4. Add spices, oregano, salt, and pepper.
5. Cook on low heat for 2 hours.
6. Garnish and serve over rice or with crusty bread.
7. Opa!
~~~~~~~~~~~~~~~~

1
person

460
calories

25
minutes

Mexican Steak Quesadillas

A fiesta in every bite! Savor the marriage of juicy steak, melted cheese, and vibrant spices, all hugged by golden tortillas.

Ingredients:

- 6 oz sirloin steak
- 2 large flour tortillas
- 1 cup shredded cheese blend
- 1/2 red bell pepper, sliced
- 1/4 red onion, sliced
- 1 tsp chili powder
- 1/2 tsp cumin
- Salt and pepper to taste
- Fresh cilantro for garnish
- Sour cream for dipping
- Salsa for serving

Directions

1. Season steak with chili powder, cumin, salt, and pepper.
2. Grill steak to medium-rare; slice thinly.
3. Place tortilla in pan; add cheese, steak, veggies.
4. Top with second tortilla; cook until golden.
5. Slice, garnish, and serve with salsa and sour cream.
6. ¡Buen provecho!

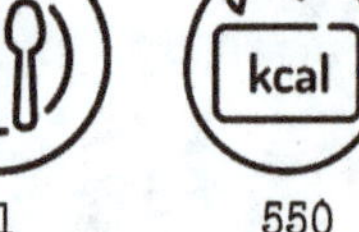

1
person

550
calories

30
minutes

Italian Marsala Wine Ribeye

Ingredients:

- 1 ribeye steak (12 oz)
- 1/2 cup Marsala wine
- 1/4 cup beef broth
- 2 tbsp butter
- 1 shallot, minced
- 2 cloves garlic, minced
- 1 tsp thyme leaves
- Salt and pepper to taste
- Fresh parsley for garnish
- Creamy polenta for serving
- Sautéed spinach for side

A velvety embrace of Marsala wine infuses this ribeye with Italian flair, a savory symphony that dances on your palate.

Directions

1. Sear steak; set aside.
2. Sauté shallots, garlic, and thyme in butter.
3. Pour in wine; reduce by half.
4. Add broth; simmer.
5. Return steak; coat in sauce.
6. Plate with polenta, spinach.
7. Garnish with parsley.
8. Buon appetito!

1
person

400
calories

18
minutes

Japanese Sesame-Garlic Sirloin

A harmony of soy, sesame, and garlic envelops tender sirloin, creating an umami-rich experience that pays homage to Japan.

Ingredients:

- 8 oz sirloin steak
- 2 tbsp soy sauce
- 1 tbsp toasted sesame oil
- 2 cloves garlic, minced
- 1 tbsp sesame seeds
- 1 green onion, sliced
- 1 tsp grated ginger
- Salt and pepper to taste
- Steamed white rice for serving
- Steamed broccoli for side

Directions

1. Combine soy sauce, sesame oil, garlic, and ginger.
2. Marinate steak; sprinkle sesame seeds.
3. Grill steak to desired doneness.
4. Rest, slice, garnish with green onion.
5. Serve over rice with steamed broccoli.
6. Itadakimasu!

1
person

470
calories

28
minutes

Brazilian Mango-Chili Glazed Picanha

Ingredients:

- 10 oz picanha steak
- 1/4 cup mango puree
- 2 tbsp lime juice
- 1 tbsp honey
- 1 tsp chili powder
- Salt and pepper to taste
- Fresh cilantro for garnish
- Rice and black beans for serving
- Grilled plantains for side

A carnival of flavors! Succulent picanha meets the sweetness of mango and the kick of chili for a Brazilian sensation.

Directions

1. Mix mango puree, lime juice, honey, and chili powder.
2. Grill steak; brush with glaze.
3. Slice, garnish, and serve with rice, beans, and plantains.
4. Saborear!

Substitutions

-

1
person

590
calories

35
minutes

Indian Beef Biryani

Embark on a fragrant passage to India with this biryani – tender beef intermingled with aromatic spices and long-grain basmati rice.

Ingredients:

- 1/2 lb beef, cubed
- 1 cup basmati rice
- 1/2 cup plain yogurt
- 1 onion, thinly sliced
- 2 cloves garlic, minced
- 1 tbsp ginger paste
- 1/2 tsp cumin
- 1/2 tsp coriander
- 1/4 tsp turmeric
- 1/4 tsp cardamom
- Saffron strands soaked in warm milk
- Cashews and raisins for garnish
- Fresh cilantro for serving

Directions

1. Marinate beef in yogurt, garlic, ginger, and spices.
2. Sauté onions; add marinated beef.
3. Layer rice, beef, saffron milk, nuts, raisins.
4. Cover and cook on low heat.
5. Garnish with cilantro.
6. Savor the flavors of India!

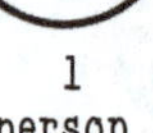

1
person

410
calories

40
minutes

Turkish Beef and Eggplant Stew (Imam Bayildi)

A slow-cooked Turkish marvel! Tender beef and luscious eggplant unite in a stew that whispers tales of Ottoman kitchens.

Ingredients:

- 1/2 lb beef stew meat
- 1 eggplant, sliced
- 1 onion, chopped
- 2 tomatoes, diced
- 3 cloves garlic, minced
- 1/4 cup olive oil
- 1/2 tsp cumin
- 1/2 tsp paprika
- 1/4 tsp cinnamon
- 1/4 tsp allspice
- Fresh parsley for garnish
- Yogurt for serving
- Turkish bread for dipping

Directions

1. Sear beef; set aside.
2. Sauté onion, garlic, and spices in oil.
3. Layer eggplant, beef, and tomatoes.
4. Cover, simmer until tender.
5. Garnish, serve with yogurt and bread.
6. Afiyet olsun!

1
person

510
calories

55
minutes

Korean Galbi Jjim (Braised Short Ribs)

Ingredients:

- 1 lb beef short ribs
- 1 Asian pear, grated
- 1/4 cup soy sauce
- 2 tbsp brown sugar
- 1 tbsp sesame oil
- 1 tbsp minced ginger
- 3 cloves garlic, minced
- 2 green onions, sliced
- 1/2 cup water
- Steamed rice for serving
- Kimchi for side

A Korean comfort embrace! Succulent short ribs stewed with soy, ginger, and Asian pear, inviting you to taste the soul of Seoul.

Directions

1. Marinate ribs in pear, soy sauce, sugar, oil, ginger, and garlic.
2. Sear ribs; add green onions and water.
3. Braise until tender.
4. Serve over rice with kimchi.
5. Mashikeh!

1
person

480
calories

22
minutes

Argentinean Beef Milanesa

Ingredients:

- 1 beef milanesa (6 oz)
- 1/2 cup breadcrumbs
- 1/4 cup grated Parmesan
- 1 egg
- 1/4 cup milk
- 2 cloves garlic, minced
- 1/2 tsp paprika
- Salt and pepper to taste
- Lemon wedges for serving
- Mashed potatoes for side

A taste of Buenos Aires! Crispy breaded beef cutlet, juicy and savory inside, pays homage to Argentina's rich culinary heritage.

Directions

1. Mix breadcrumbs, Parmesan, garlic, and paprika.
2. Dip milanesa in egg-milk mixture, coat with breadcrumbs.
3. Fry until golden.
4. Serve with mashed potatoes and lemon wedges.
5. ¡Buen provecho!

Chapter 9:
Global Steak Bowls

 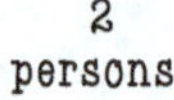  

2
persons

320/ser
ving

25
minutes

Thai Basil Beef Stir-Fry Bowl

Straight from the bustling streets of Bangkok, this bowl is a symphony of aromatics. Tender beef dances with Thai basil, chili, and garlic—a stir-fry that's a taste of Thailand's vibrant energy.

Ingredients:

- 1 lb beef sirloin, thinly sliced
- 2 cups jasmine rice, cooked
- 2 tbsp vegetable oil
- 3 cloves garlic, minced
- 2 Thai bird's eye chilies, chopped
- ½ cup Thai basil leaves
- 2 tbsp oyster sauce
- 1 tbsp soy sauce
- Lime wedges for serving

Directions

1. Heat oil in a wok.
2. Sauté garlic, chilies until fragrant.
3. Add beef, stir-fry until cooked.
4. Add oyster sauce, soy sauce.
5. Toss in basil leaves.
6. Serve over rice.
7. Garnish with lime.

1
person

280/ser
ving

30
minutes

Greek Beef Souvlaki Bowl

Ingredients:

- 1 skewer of beef souvlaki
- 1 cup cooked quinoa
- ½ cup cherry tomatoes, halved
- ¼ cup Kalamata olives, pitted
- 2 tbsp feta cheese, crumbled
- Red onion slices
- Tzatziki sauce for drizzling

From the sun-soaked shores of Greece, this bowl is a melody of flavors. Grilled beef souvlaki, nestled on a bed of Mediterranean treasures—olives, tomatoes, and feta—an ode to Greek indulgence.

Directions

1. Grill souvlaki skewer until charred.
2. Assemble quinoa, tomatoes, olives, feta.
3. Top with souvlaki.
4. Drizzle with tzatziki.
5. Garnish with red onion.

1
person

360/ser
ving

20
minutes

Mexican Steak Burrito Bowl

Ingredients:

- 1 cup cooked rice
- 1 grilled steak, sliced
- ½ cup black beans, drained
- ½ cup corn kernels
- ½ cup salsa
- ½ avocado, sliced
- ¼ cup shredded cheddar cheese
- Fresh cilantro for garnish

A fiesta of flavors, this burrito bowl is a Tex-Mex delight. Grilled steak meets vibrant salsa, black beans, and avocado—a tribute to the lively spirit of Mexican cuisine.

Directions

1. Layer rice, steak, beans, corn, salsa.
2. Top with avocado, cheese.
3. Garnish with cilantro.

2
persons

380/ser
ving

40
minutes

Italian Steak and Mushroom Risotto Bowl

Ingredients:

- 1 lb beef striploin, sliced
- 1 cup Arborio rice
- ½ cup white wine
- 4 cups beef broth
- 1 cup mushrooms, sliced
- ½ onion, chopped
- 2 cloves garlic, minced
- ¼ cup Parmesan cheese
- Fresh parsley for garnish

From the heart of Italy, this risotto bowl is a symphony of comfort. Tender steak and earthy mushrooms embrace creamy risotto—a culinary embrace that harks back to Roman trattorias.

Directions

1. Sear steak until desired doneness.
2. Sauté mushrooms, onion, garlic.
3. Add rice, wine, broth.
4. Cook risotto until creamy.
5. Stir in cheese.
6. Serve steak over risotto.
7. Garnish with parsley.

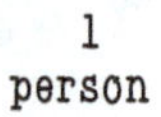

1
person

310/ser
ving

35
minutes

Japanese Teriyaki Steak Bowl

Ingredients:

- 1 ribeye steak, grilled and sliced
- 1 cup steamed sushi rice
- ½ cup broccoli florets, steamed
- ½ cup carrot, julienned and blanched
- ½ cup edamame, steamed
- Teriyaki sauce for drizzling

A slice of Tokyo's culinary flair, this bowl captures Japan's balance of flavors. Grilled teriyaki steak, nestled on a bed of steamed rice with vibrant vegetables—a taste of Japanese harmony.

Directions

1. Grill steak, slice.
2. Assemble rice, veggies.
3. Top with steak.
4. Drizzle with teriyaki sauce.

2
persons

290/ser
ving

30
minutes

Korean Bulgogi Bowl with Sirloin

Ingredients:

- 1 lb beef sirloin, thinly sliced
- 2 cups cooked rice
- ½ cup carrots, julienned
- ½ cup cucumber, sliced
- ½ cup red cabbage, shredded
- 2 green onions, chopped
- Sesame seeds for garnish

Seoul's vibrant spirit shines in this bowl. Thinly sliced sirloin, marinated in a blend of soy, ginger, and garlic, meets a colorful array of vegetables—a harmonious Korean culinary experience.

Directions

1. Marinate steak in soy, ginger, garlic.
2. Sear until cooked.
3. Assemble rice, veggies.
4. Top with steak.
5. Garnish with green onions, sesame seeds.

1
person

320/ser
ving

40
minutes

Turkish Beef Pide Bowl

Ingredients:

- 1 portion beef pide
- ½ cup ground beef mixture
- ½ cup tomatoes, chopped
- ¼ cup red bell pepper, chopped
- ¼ cup green bell pepper, chopped
- ¼ cup red onion, chopped
- ½ cup Greek yogurt
- Sumac for garnish

From the shores of the Bosphorus, this bowl is a Turkish delight. Ground beef, fragrant with spices, meets warm pide bread, yogurt, and a symphony of Mediterranean flavors.

Directions

1. Bake pide with beef mixture, tomatoes, peppers, onion.
2. Serve with yogurt.
3. Garnish with sumac.

1
person

350/ser
ving

30
minutes

Argentinean Chimichurri Steak Bowl

A tribute to the Argentinian plains, this bowl is a tango of flavors. Grilled steak, slathered in vibrant chimichurri sauce, meets fluffy rice, beans, and roasted red peppers.

Ingredients:

- 1 grilled steak, sliced
- 1 cup cooked rice
- ½ cup black beans, cooked
- ½ cup roasted red peppers, sliced
- Chimichurri sauce for drizzling
- Fresh parsley for garnish

Directions

1. Grill steak, slice.
2. Assemble rice, beans, peppers.
3. Top with steak.
4. Drizzle with chimichurri.
5. Garnish with parsley.

2
persons

300/ser
ving

45
minutes

Indian Beef Kofta Curry Bowl

Ingredients:

- 1 lb beef kofta
- 2 cups cooked basmati rice
- 1 cup tomato curry sauce
- Fresh cilantro for garnish

A journey to India's spice markets, this bowl is a curry-filled delight. Beef kofta, infused with aromatic spices, swim in a rich tomato curry—a symphony of Indian flavors on your plate.

Directions

1. Sear kofta until cooked.
2. Heat curry sauce.
3. Serve kofta over rice.
4. Drizzle with sauce.
5. Garnish with cilantro.

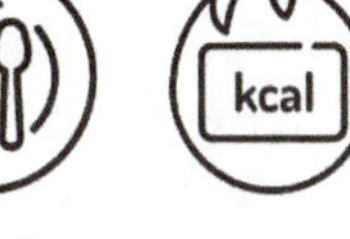

1
person

380/ser
ving

50
minutes

Brazilian Feijoada Bowl with Beef

Ingredients:

- 1 cup beef feijoada
- 1 cup cooked white rice
- ½ orange, sliced
- Farofa (toasted cassava flour) for sprinkling

Straight from Rio's samba-filled streets, this bowl is a carnival of flavors. Hearty beef feijoada, a symphony of black beans, sausage, and spices, sings of Brazil's festive spirit.

Directions

1. Warm feijoada.
2. Assemble rice, feijoada.
3. Top with orange slices.
4. Sprinkle with farofa.

Chapter 10:
Exotic Steak
Adventures

2
persons

340/ser
ving

30
minutes

Chinese Five-Spice Peppered Sirloin

Ingredients:

- 1 lb beef sirloin, sliced
- 2 cups mixed stir-fry vegetables
- 2 tbsp soy sauce
- 1 tsp Chinese five-spice powder
- 1 tsp black pepper
- 2 cloves garlic, minced
- 1 tsp ginger, minced
- 2 green onions, chopped
- Sesame seeds for garnish

A journey along the Great Wall—this dish is a fusion of flavors. Five-spice-kissed sirloin, stir-fried with vibrant vegetables, dances in your mouth like a Chinese dragon.

Directions

1. Marinate steak in soy sauce, five-spice, pepper.
2. Stir-fry garlic, ginger.
3. Add steak, vegetables.
4. Toss until cooked.
5. Top with green onions, sesame seeds.

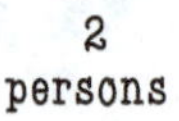

2
persons

360/ser
ving

40
minutes

Peruvian Lomo Saltado with Sirloin

Ingredients:

- 1 lb beef sirloin, sliced
- 2 cups cooked French fries
- 1 red onion, sliced
- 2 tomatoes, sliced
- ½ cup soy sauce
- ¼ cup vinegar
- 2 cloves garlic, minced
- 1 tsp cumin
- ½ cup fresh cilantro, chopped

From the Andes to your plate, this dish is a Peruvian masterpiece. Sirloin, sautéed with onions, tomatoes, and fries, carries the warmth of South America's rich culinary heritage.

Directions

1. Sauté onion, garlic until softened.
2. Add steak, cumin.
3. Stir in soy sauce, vinegar.
4. Toss in tomatoes.
5. Serve over fries.
6. Garnish with cilantro.

1
person

320/ser
ving

35
minutes

Vietnamese Lemongrass Beef Bánh Mì

Ingredients:

- 1 baguette or French roll
- 1 portion lemongrass beef
- ½ cup pickled daikon and carrots
- Fresh cilantro, mint, basil leaves
- Sliced jalapeños
- Hoisin and Sriracha sauce for drizzling

A Saigon street feast captured in a bowl. Lemongrass-marinated beef, nestled in a bed of pickled daikon, carrots, and fresh herbs, is Vietnam's ode to balance and fresh flavors.

Directions

1. Grill lemongrass beef until charred.
2. Warm baguette.
3. Assemble beef, pickled veggies.
4. Top with herbs, jalapeños.
5. Drizzle with hoisin, Sriracha.

2
persons

340/ser
ving

30
minutes

Thai Beef Pad See Ew

Ingredients:

- 1 lb beef sirloin, thinly sliced
- 8 oz wide rice noodles
- 2 cups broccoli florets, blanched
- 3 cloves garlic, minced
- 2 eggs
- ¼ cup soy sauce
- 2 tbsp oyster sauce
- 1 tsp sugar
- Crushed red pepper flakes for heat

From Bangkok's bustling markets, this dish is a Thai delight. Tender beef, wide rice noodles, and broccoli waltz in a sweet soy sauce—an invitation to savor Thailand's street flavors.

Directions

1. Sear beef, garlic until cooked.
2. Push aside, scramble eggs.
3. Add noodles, sauces, sugar.
4. Toss in beef, broccoli.
5. Sprinkle with red pepper flakes.

2
persons

370/ser
ving

50
minutes

Indonesian Rendang Sirloin

Ingredients:

- 1 lb beef sirloin, cubed
- 1 can coconut milk
- 2 stalks lemongrass, bruised
- 3 kaffir lime leaves
- 2 cloves garlic, minced
- 1 tsp ginger, minced
- 2 tbsp rendang curry paste
- 1 tsp tamarind paste
- Fresh cilantro for garnish

From Indonesia's tropical embrace, this dish is a symphony of flavors. Rendang-spiced sirloin, slow-cooked in coconut milk and spices, captures the heart of Indonesian culinary art.

Directions

1. Sear beef, garlic, ginger.
2. Add curry paste, coconut milk, tamarind.
3. Simmer with lemongrass, lime leaves.
4. Cook until tender.
5. Garnish with cilantro.

 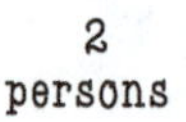  

2
persons

320/ser
ving

40
minutes

Ethiopian Key Wat Spiced Steak

Ingredients:

- 1 lb beef sirloin, cubed
- 1 cup berbere sauce
- 1 onion, chopped
- 2 cloves garlic, minced
- 1 tsp ginger, minced
- 2 cups beef broth
- Injera or rice for serving

From the highlands of Ethiopia, this dish is a culinary journey. Spiced steak, slow-cooked in rich berbere sauce, carries the warmth of African spices and the heart of Ethiopian culture.

Directions

1. Sear beef, onion, garlic, ginger.
2. Add berbere sauce, beef broth.
3. Simmer until tender.
4. Serve with injera or rice.

1
person

360/ser
ving

30
minutes

Australian Outback Steakhouse Style

Ingredients:

- 1 ribeye steak, grilled
- 1 portion seasoned fries
- Mixed greens salad with tomatoes, cucumber, red onion
- Choice of dressing

A taste of the outback—this dish is Australia on a plate. Flame-grilled steak, loaded with seasoned fries and a fresh salad, captures the hearty spirit of Down Under dining.

Directions

1. Grill steak to desired doneness.
2. Serve with fries.
3. Plate with mixed greens.
4. Drizzle with dressing.

2
persons

kcal

330/ser
ving

40
minutes

Russian Beef Stroganoff

Ingredients:

- 1 lb beef sirloin, thinly sliced
- 2 cups sliced mushrooms
- 1 onion, chopped
- 2 cloves garlic, minced
- ½ cup sour cream
- ½ cup beef broth
- 2 tbsp Dijon mustard
- 2 tbsp fresh dill, chopped
- Cooked egg noodles for serving

A taste of Russian nobility—this dish is a symphony of flavors. Tender beef, sautéed with mushrooms and onions, dances in a creamy sauce, carrying the elegance of St. Petersburg.

Directions

1. Sauté beef, mushrooms, onion, garlic.
2. Stir in sour cream, beef broth.
3. Add Dijon mustard, dill.
4. Simmer until creamy.
5. Serve over egg noodles.

1
person

310/ser
ving

35
minutes

Middle Eastern Shawarma-Style Skirt Steak

Ingredients:

- 1 skirt steak, marinated in shawarma spices
- 1 cup mixed vegetables (bell peppers, tomatoes, onions)
- ½ cup Greek yogurt
- Fresh parsley, mint for garnish
- Pita bread for serving

A journey through Middle Eastern markets, this dish is a sensory delight. Skirt steak, marinated in shawarma spices, meets a colorful array of vegetables, yogurt, and pita—an invitation to feast.

Directions

1. Grill steak until charred.
2. Sauté vegetables until tender.
3. Serve steak with veggies, yogurt.
4. Garnish with herbs.
5. Serve with pita.

1
person

380/ser
ving

50
minutes

Scottish Steak and Ale Pie

Ingredients:

- 1 portion beef stew with ale gravy
- Prepared puff pastry
- 1 egg, beaten (for egg wash)
- Mashed potatoes or vegetables for serving

From the highlands of Scotland, this dish is a cozy embrace. Tender beef, slow-cooked in ale gravy, is nestled beneath a flaky pastry—a warm tribute to Scotland's hearty traditions.

Directions

1. Warm beef stew.
2. Transfer to oven-safe dish.
3. Top with puff pastry.
4. Brush with egg wash.
5. Bake until golden.
6. Serve with mashed potatoes or vegetables.

Chapter 11:
Innovative Steak Dishes

 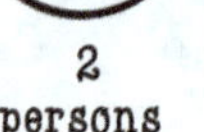

2
persons

**400/ser
ving**

45
minutes

Japanese Kobe Beef Sushi Rolls

Ingredients:

- 8 slices Kobe beef (thinly sliced)
- 2 sheets nori
- 1 cup sushi rice, cooked and seasoned
- ½ cucumber, julienned
- ½ avocado, sliced
- Soy sauce and wasabi for dipping

The epitome of luxury—these rolls are a harmonious blend of Japanese elegance. Melt-in-your-mouth Kobe beef, paired with fresh cucumber and avocado, wrapped in nori and sushi rice.

Directions

1. Lay nori on bamboo mat.
2. Spread rice on nori, leaving space.
3. Arrange Kobe beef, cucumber, avocado.
4. Roll tightly.
5. Slice into rolls.
6. Serve with soy sauce and wasabi.

1
person

420/ser
ving

40
minutes

French Tournedos Rossini

Ingredients:

- 1 tournedos steak
- 1 slice foie gras
- 1 slice brioche
- 2 tbsp truffle oil
- 2 tbsp red wine reduction
- Salt and pepper
- Fresh thyme for garnish

A culinary masterpiece, this dish is a tribute to French decadence. Tender tournedos of beef, seared and topped with foie gras, all resting on a delicate slice of brioche.

Directions

1. Season steak with salt and pepper.
2. Sear until desired doneness.
3. Sear foie gras.
4. Toast brioche.
5. Assemble brioche, steak, foie gras.
6. Drizzle with truffle oil, wine reduction.
7. Garnish with thyme.

4
persons

350/ser
ving

50
minutes

Mexican Steak Chili

A fiesta of flavors in every bite, this chili is a blend of Tex-Mex comfort. Tender steak, black beans, tomatoes, and spices unite in a hearty bowl —a culinary celebration of Mexico.

Ingredients:

- 1 lb beef sirloin, cubed
- 1 can black beans, drained
- 1 can diced tomatoes
- 1 onion, chopped
- 2 cloves garlic, minced
- 2 tbsp chili powder
- 1 tsp cumin
- 1 tsp paprika
- Sour cream and shredded cheese for topping

Directions

1. Sauté onion, garlic until softened.
2. Add beef, spices, cook until browned.
3. Add tomatoes, beans.
4. Simmer until flavors meld.
5. Serve topped with sour cream and cheese.

2
persons

380/ser
ving

40
minutes

Thai Pineapple Beef Fried Rice

Ingredients:

- 1 lb beef sirloin, thinly sliced
- 2 cups cooked jasmine rice
- 1 cup fresh pineapple, diced
- 1 cup mixed vegetables (peas, carrots, bell peppers)
- 2 eggs
- 2 tbsp soy sauce
- Fresh cilantro for garnish

A symphony of sweet and savory, this dish captures Thailand's vibrant flavors. Tender beef, fresh pineapple, and fragrant herbs waltz in a wok of fragrant jasmine rice.

Directions

1. Sear beef until cooked.
2. Push aside, scramble eggs.
3. Add vegetables, rice.
4. Toss in beef, pineapple.
5. Stir in soy sauce.
6. Garnish with cilantro.

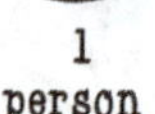

1
person

360/ser
ving

45
minutes

Turkish Beef Iskender Kebab

Ingredients:

- 1 portion Iskender-style beef
- 1 piece pita bread
- ½ cup tomato sauce
- ½ cup yogurt
- Fresh parsley for garnish
- Sumac for sprinkling

A taste of Istanbul's street food culture, this dish is a journey through Turkey's rich flavors. Thinly sliced beef, layered over pita, and drizzled with tomato sauce and yogurt.

Directions

1. Warm pita bread.
2. Arrange beef over pita.
3. Drizzle with tomato sauce.
4. Top with yogurt.
5. Garnish with parsley and sumac.

2
persons

kcal
300/ser
ving

30
minutes

Italian Beef Carpaccio

A work of culinary art, this dish is a canvas of flavors. Paper-thin beef slices, drizzled with olive oil and lemon, crowned with arugula and Parmesan —Italy's ode to simplicity.

Ingredients:

- 8 oz beef tenderloin, thinly sliced
- 2 cups arugula
- ½ cup shaved Parmesan cheese
- 2 tbsp extra-virgin olive oil
- 1 lemon, zest and juice
- Salt and pepper

Directions

1. Arrange beef slices on a plate.
2. Toss arugula with olive oil, lemon juice, zest.
3. Place arugula over beef.
4. Top with Parmesan.
5. Drizzle with more olive oil.
6. Season with salt and pepper.

1
person

380/ser
ving

35
minutes

Korean Bulgogi Burger

Ingredients:

- 1 beef burger patty
- 1 sesame burger bun
- 2 tbsp bulgogi marinade
- ¼ cup Asian slaw (cabbage, carrots, green onions)
- 1 tbsp sesame seeds
- Sriracha mayo for spreading

A fusion of East and West, this burger is a burst of flavors. Beef patty, marinated in savory-sweet bulgogi sauce, meets a sesame bun and a colorful slaw—a taste of Seoul's culinary flair.

Directions

1. Marinate patty in bulgogi sauce.
2. Grill until cooked.
3. Toast bun.
4. Assemble burger with slaw.
5. Spread Sriracha mayo.
6. Sprinkle with sesame seeds.

2
persons

340/ser
ving

40
minutes

Brazilian Picanha Pão de Queijo Sliders

Ingredients:

- 2 mini pão de queijo buns
- 1 portion grilled picanha
- ½ cup mixed greens
- 2 slices tomato
- Chimichurri sauce for spreading

A taste of Brazil's vibrancy, these sliders are a carnival of flavors. Grilled picanha, nestled in cheesy pão de queijo buns, embraces the spirit of Brazilian street food.

Directions

1. Warm pão de queijo buns.
2. Assemble with greens, tomato.
3. Layer grilled picanha.
4. Spread chimichurri sauce.

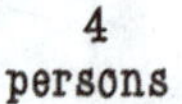

4
persons

290/ser
ving

30
minutes

Indian Beef Seekh Kebabs

Ingredients:

- 1 lb ground beef
- 1 onion, finely chopped
- 2 cloves garlic, minced
- 1 tsp ginger, minced
- 1 tbsp ground coriander
- 1 tbsp ground cumin
- 1 tsp chili powder
- Fresh cilantro for garnish

A fragrant journey through India's flavors, these kebabs are a blend of spices and succulence. Minced beef, seasoned with aromatic spices, skewered and grilled to perfection.

Directions

1. Mix beef, onion, garlic, ginger, spices.
2. Shape into kebabs on skewers.
3. Grill until cooked.
4. Garnish with cilantro.

2
persons

370/ser
ving

50
minutes

Argentinean Beef Empanadas

Ingredients:

- 4 beef empanadas
- 1 portion seasoned beef filling
- Salsa criolla (tomato and onion salsa) for dipping

Straight from Buenos Aires, these empanadas are a taste of Argentina's soul. Flaky pastry pockets, stuffed with seasoned beef, olives, and raisins, carry the warmth of Argentine kitchens.

Directions

1. Warm empanadas.
2. Serve with seasoned beef filling.
3. Dip in salsa criolla.

Substitutions

Chapter 12:
Surprising Steak Sides

2
persons

320/ser
ving

25
minutes

Japanese Garlic Fried Rice with Steak

A Tokyo-inspired side, this rice is a symphony of flavors. Tender steak, garlic-infused fried rice, and a touch of soy sauce—Japan's culinary finesse in every fragrant bite.

Ingredients:

- 1 cup cooked Japanese short-grain rice
- 1 portion garlic fried rice with steak
- 1 tbsp soy sauce
- 1 tsp sesame oil
- 2 green onions, chopped
- Sesame seeds for garnish

Directions

1. Warm cooked rice.
2. Mix with garlic fried rice.
3. Drizzle with soy sauce, sesame oil.
4. Toss in green onions.
5. Sprinkle with sesame seeds.

1
person

310/ser
ving

30
minutes

Greek Tzatziki and Steak Pita Pockets

Ingredients:

- 1 pita pocket
- 1 portion grilled steak
- ¼ cup Tzatziki sauce
- Mixed greens
- Sliced cucumber and tomato

From the Greek isles, these pockets are a taste of Mediterranean delight. Grilled steak, crisp veggies, and creamy tzatziki tucked into warm pita—a culinary journey to the Aegean.

Directions

1. Warm pita pocket.
2. Spread Tzatziki inside.
3. Layer grilled steak, greens, cucumber, and tomato.
4. Fold and enjoy.

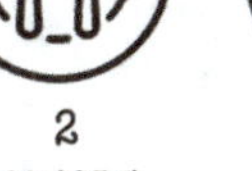

2
persons

280/ser ving

35
minutes

Mexican Elote-Style Corn and Steak

A taste of Mexican street food, this side is a fiesta of flavors. Grilled steak, slathered with elote-style corn (creamy mayo, chili, and cheese), embodies the spirit of Mexico.

Ingredients:

- 1 portion grilled steak
- 2 ears of corn, grilled and slathered with elote-style toppings (mayo, chili powder, cotija cheese)
- Fresh lime wedges

Directions

1. Grill steak until cooked.
2. Grill corn, slather with toppings.
3. Serve with lime wedges.

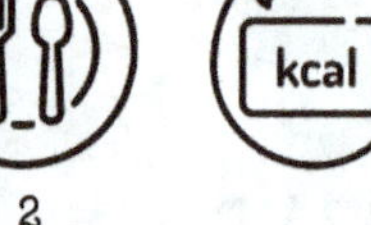

2
persons

290/ser ving

20
minutes

Italian Caprese Salad with Steak

Ingredients:

- 1 portion grilled steak
- 1 large tomato, sliced
- Fresh mozzarella cheese, sliced
- Fresh basil leaves
- Balsamic vinegar
- Extra-virgin olive oil
- Salt and pepper

A taste of Italy's summer, this salad is a colorful ode to simplicity. Grilled steak, fresh tomatoes, mozzarella, basil, and a drizzle of balsamic—a taste of la dolce vita.

Directions

1. Grill steak until cooked.
2. Assemble tomato, mozzarella, and basil on a plate.
3. Top with steak slices.
4. Drizzle with balsamic vinegar and olive oil.
5. Season with salt and pepper.

2
persons

320/ser
ving

30
minutes

Korean Kimchi Steak Fried Rice

Ingredients:

- 1 portion grilled steak
- 2 cups cooked jasmine rice
- ½ cup kimchi, chopped
- 2 eggs
- 1 tsp sesame oil
- 2 green onions, chopped
- Sesame seeds for garnish

Seoul's flavors come alive in this side. Grilled steak, vibrant kimchi, and fragrant fried rice dance in your mouth—a taste of Korea's dynamic culinary palette.

Directions

1. Grill steak until cooked.
2. Push aside, scramble eggs.
3. Add rice, kimchi.
4. Toss in steak slices.
5. Stir in sesame oil.
6. Garnish with green onions and sesame seeds.

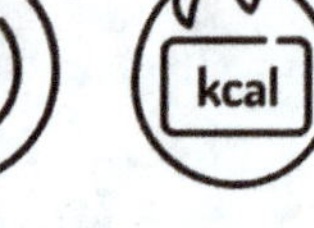

2 persons

300/ser ving

35 minutes

Turkish Grilled Eggplant and Steak Stacks

Ingredients:

- 1 portion grilled steak
- 1 large eggplant, sliced and grilled
- ½ cup Greek yogurt
- Fresh parsley, chopped
- Sumac for sprinkling

A taste of the Bosphorus, this side is a symphony of textures. Grilled steak, creamy eggplant, and tangy yogurt come together—a culinary journey through Turkey's soul.

Directions

1. Grill steak until cooked.
2. Grill eggplant slices.
3. Stack eggplant and steak.
4. Top with Greek yogurt.
5. Garnish with parsley and sumac.

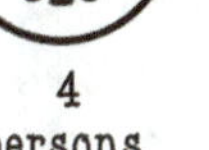

4
persons

280/ser
ving

45
minutes

Indian Spiced Steak Samosas

Ingredients:

- 1 portion spiced steak filling
- 8 samosa pastry sheets
- Oil for frying

An Indian twist to samosas, this side is a burst of flavors. Spiced steak, onions, and peas are tucked into crispy pastry pockets—a journey through India's street food culture.

Directions

1. Fill samosa pastry sheets with spiced steak filling.
2. Seal and fold into samosa shape.
3. Deep-fry until golden and crispy.

2
persons

270/ser
ving

25
minutes

Brazilian Steak and Black Bean Salad

Ingredients:

- 1 portion grilled steak
- 1 cup black beans, cooked
- Mixed greens
- Cherry tomatoes, halved
- Red onion, thinly sliced
- Fresh cilantro, chopped
- Lime dressing

A tribute to Brazil's vibrant flavors, this salad is a dance of textures. Grilled steak, black beans, crisp vegetables, and zesty lime dressing—a taste of South American vitality.

Directions

1. Grill steak until cooked.
2. Toss black beans, greens, tomatoes, and onion.
3. Top with steak slices.
4. Drizzle with lime dressing.
5. Garnish with cilantro.

2
persons

290/ser
ving

30
minutes

Thai Papaya Salad with Grilled Beef

Ingredients:

- 1 portion grilled beef
- 2 cups shredded green papaya
- ¼ cup shredded carrots
- ¼ cup peanuts, chopped
- Fresh cilantro, chopped
- Thai chili-lime dressing

A taste of Bangkok's street markets, this salad is a burst of flavors. Grilled beef, shredded papaya, and zesty dressing dance in harmony—a culinary journey to Thailand's heart.

Directions

1. Grill steak until cooked.
2. Toss papaya, carrots, and peanuts.
3. Top with steak slices.
4. Drizzle with Thai chili-lime dressing.
5. Garnish with cilantro.

2
persons

**300/ser
ving**

25
minutes

Argentinean Steak Chimichurri Salad

Ingredients:

- 1 portion grilled steak
- Mixed greens
- Cherry tomatoes, halved
- Red onion, thinly sliced
- Chimichurri sauce

From the streets of Buenos Aires, this salad is a symphony of flavors. Grilled steak, fresh greens, and tangy chimichurri sauce embody the soul of Argentinean culinary art.

Directions

1. Grill steak until cooked.
2. Toss greens, tomatoes, and onion.
3. Top with steak slices.
4. Drizzle with chimichurri sauce.

Asking for Support

As our steak adventure comes to a close, a heartfelt thank you for joining us. But before we part ways, a small request.

Reviews, fellow foodies, are the heartbeat of our journey. If you've savored these recipes, could you spare a moment to share your thoughts?

You know the drill – that review button awaits. A star rating, a brief sentence – these tiny gestures mean the world.

Why reviews matter? We're a small team, fueled by culinary passion, not big budgets. Your reviews guide us, your words inspire us.

Every review is a spark of connection. Imagine us, huddled around screens, celebrating the shared love of food.

About those hiccups – we're human. Despite our best, a typo might sneak through. I hope you'll focus on the flavors we've shared.

Before we part, consider leaving a review. Your presence, your voice – they matter. Every review is read with gratitude.

As we close this chapter, remember the flavors we've savored. Your review, in words or thoughts, fuels our journey. Thank you for being part of this adventure. Until our culinary paths cross again, your support is the magic ingredient. Bon appétit!